Royal
Horticultural
Society

GROW YOUR OWN VEG

Royal
Horticultural
Society

GROW YOUR OWN **VEG**

Carol Klein

MITCHELL BEAZLEY

This book is published by Mitchell Beazley, an imprint of the
Octopus Publishing Group Ltd to accompany the television series
Grow Your Own Veg which is produced by the BBC in association
with The Royal Horticultural Society

Octopus Publishing Group Ltd is an Hachette Livre UK Company
www.hachettelivre.co.uk

Reprinted 2007 (twice) and 2008

Executive Producer Sarah Moors

Series Producer Juliet Glaves

Horticultural Researcher Phil McCann

Special thanks to photographer Jane Sebire

ISBN 9781845332938

A CIP record of this book is available from the British Library

Set in Frutiger

Printed and bound in Spain

Contents

Why grow your own?

In a world where we are becoming increasingly alienated from what we eat, growing our own vegetables is a fundamental way to reassert the connection between ourselves and our food. There is nothing more important to our wellbeing than what we eat. "You are what you eat" may be an old adage, but it makes a very topical, valid point. When you grow your own you know exactly what's in and on your vegetables.

Supermarket selections

We all know vegetables are good for us, but what a difference there is between those we buy and those we grow. Bought vegetables are selected for uniformity and their ability to be packaged neatly to fit supermarket shelves. Their production and distribution is governed by logistics often on a global scale. Vegetables are shipped and transported around the world and up and down the country. They may be kept in cold store, irradiated, washed in chlorine to destroy bacteria and treated with preservatives to prolong their shelf-life. Plant breeders' priorities are to produce crops with high yields that ripen simultaneously so machines can move in with the greatest efficiency and harvest the lot. But when convenience is everything, freshness, taste, choice and seasonality often go out of the window.

Year-round fresh food

In real life, you don't want all your vegetables to mature at the same time. By growing your own you can stagger your sowings to lengthen the season and deliberately select varieties that offer their leaves, roots or seedpods and fruits over a long period. With a bit of planning, gluts and thin times need not occur.

Fresh vegetables throughout the year should be the main aim of growing your own, but in their own season. Who wants to be eating baby sweetcorn flown in from Kenya or Peru in the middle of winter? This is the time for leeks and carrots, swedes and potatoes. In the summer you can concentrate on picking fresh, while on cold winter days, you can rely on stored roots like chunky pumpkins and potatoes, or hardy customers like leeks and parsnips.

Taking charge

When you grow your own you know exactly what's been done to each vegetable at every stage of its existence. If you grow organically, you know that it is a combination of humus-rich soil, water and perhaps an occasional feed with comfrey water or liquid seaweed that has made your vegetables grow and flourish.

One of the great advantages of growing your own vegetables is that you get the final say not only on which crops to grow but, just as importantly, which varieties to grow. On your own plot you can produce unusual vegetables that supermarkets don't stock. Try asking for fresh borlotti beans or summer squashes at your local supermarket and see what response you get. There are also many different varieties of vegetables that you never see in the shops, with a fascinating range of different flavours, colours and shapes to choose from. There is now enormous interest in heritage varieties and it is fascinating to find the ones that have merit, and then to grow them, eat them and save seed to pass on to others.

TENDING YOUR OWN vegetables will bring you into contact with the seasons and the natural rhythms of life, heightening your awareness of nature.

ABOVE: THERE IS GREAT JOY to be had in planting your crops and watching them grow to harvest. It's good for your soul.

Good for you

When you harvest your crops they are totally fresh and taste completely different to shop-bought produce. The only distance they've travelled is from the plot to the table so there are no food miles involved – only food inches. Eating fresh vegetables just pulled from the ground or picked from the plant is incredibly good for you because the fresher they are, the more packed with minerals and vitamins they're going to be. And don't forget that growing your own means working outside too, providing invaluable exercise.

But it's not just your physical health that's improved by growing and eating your own. It is immensely good for the soul – therapeutic in every way. One of the greatest joys of harvesting your own crops is to feel part of the real, natural world around you. Gardening of any kind provides an opportunity to re-establish a relationship with the soil. Putting back what you take out by feeding the soil makes you an active participant – albeit a tiny one in the earth's story. Modern living often erases the link we have with the earth or at least disguises it so much that we can't see or feel it any more. Yet growing food has been the most basic common activity of every civilization. It is fundamental to human existence and to get back down to earth re-establishes our roots.

Cycles of life

To watch the drama of the seasons unfold and to be directly affected by it through what we grow builds a deep connection with the real world. You feel the sunshine on your face as you tend and water, and watch the swallows getting ready to depart as you harvest. You experience the nip in the air as you prepare the plot for the coming year and experience the urgent resurgence of spring's vital force as seeds are sown and growth commences. You feel part of

GROWING IN HARMONY – THREE SISTERS BEDS

Native Americans planted beans between maize and we have used them as one of the three sisters in our own 'three sisters bed'. In so doing, we are emulating a practice used by Iroquois women when their three most important staple crops – beans, maize and squash – were grown together in a perfect symbiotic relationship.

The women of the tribe were the gardeners and produced most of the food, the men supplementing the vegetables with an occasional deer. The women would walk the ground gathering the soil into a series of mounds a stride apart. In the top of each mound they planted a seed of maize, two weeks later the soil would be drawn up further and a bean seed would be pushed in beside the maize. When both had germinated and started to grow, in would go a squash seed at the foot of the hollow created by building the mound.

As the corn grew, the bean would use it for support whilst at the same time fixing nitrogen in the soil and feeding itself, the corn and also the squash. Meanwhile the squash would benefit from the cool conditions created by the other two whilst spreading its stems hither and thither, its large leaves suppressing weeds and retaining moisture. All three grew up together benefiting from their relationship and producing fruitful crops. It is a perfect example of people growing in harmony with the land.

the cycle of the growing year. So much of life is controlled by arbitrary notions of time – financial years, school holidays, and paying the mortgage or the rent. Growing your own presents you with a more meaningful measure of time – the full circle from sowing seed to eating what you have grown, and then collecting your own seed and starting all over again is what life is really all about.

Glebe Cottage

We have lived at Glebe Cottage for almost 30 years and I've run my nursery business from there for 25 of them. The garden is long, on a south-facing slope nestling into the side of a hill. The soil is heavy clay, hard work – but very fertile. We moved here to escape city life to look for something closer to the earth. We had two daughters Annie and Alice and decided we wanted to feed ourselves so we grew lots

of veg and fruit for the first few years. However, eventually raising plants for the nursery and flower shows had to take priority but I always wanted to get back to organic veg gardening and, now the girls are grown up and the nursery is well-established, I've had the opportunity to grow my own on two small plots within the garden. We garden wholly organically. We do not use chemicals, pesticides, herbicides, fungicides or peat, as we emphasise in the BBC TV programmes.

When you grow your own vegetables you know the only distance they've travelled is from the plot to the table and you know they're absolutely fresh. It's huge fun too but above all it's the taste that's so irresistible.

BELOW: YOU CAN SEE from this immaculate onion bed that weeding is easy when they are at table-top height. My onions have grown plump from the extra care and lack of competition.

Preparation and techniques

- Growing in a small space
- Know your plot
- Preparing the plot
- All about growing
- Extending the season
- Coping with problems
- Planning what to grow

Growing in a small space

For the increasing number of people wanting to grow vegetables at home, the first big question is, 'Will I have room?'. The answer is, 'Yes'. It is perfectly possible to grow vegetables in anything from a window box or tub to a raised bed, and it's not essential to have a large greenhouse or polytunnel. A small area means you can grow small numbers of lots of different crops.

Making a raised bed

A raised bed in the garden or on a patio can increase the range and quantity of vegetables grown. Traditionally, vegetables were grown in long rows on flat soil, with the space between the crops giving easy access for harvesting. In a raised bed (think of it as a large, specially constructed container with no base), the growing area is higher than the ground, and its sides are usually made of wood or brick, the choice depending on cost, looks and available materials. Ready-to-assemble DIY raised beds are a good option, but tend to be more expensive.

At the RHS garden at Harlow Carr, in Harrogate, a raised bed was built on a 3 x 3m (10 x 10ft) plot to demonstrate what is possible in a small area. Two areas were created – a 1.2 x 1.2m (4 x 4ft) square bed for salads and herbs, and a larger L-shaped area for other vegetables – separated by a 60cm (24in) wide path. The path gives easy access in all weathers, and means the cultivated soil isn't compacted under foot.

ADVANTAGES OF A RAISED BED

• The growing area is concentrated in a permanent bed with easy access from a permanent path.

• The soil dries out and warms up quite quickly. This is an advantage on cold wet clay, and where spring can be late. Also, the plot can be worked on for more days of the year, and in poor weather.

• It's possible to plant closer and get good yields, even on small beds, because the planting and sowing are concentrated in deep soil with high fertility, and there is extra light from the sides. The paths also give good access, so the soil won't be compacted by treading, thereby damaging its structure, hindering drainage, and make it harder to warm up in spring.

• There is ample growing depth, which is especially useful for root vegetables.

• You can fill the raised bed with the most appropriate soil for your crop.

• One raised bed is a much less daunting prospect than a large vegetable plot which needs planning, planting and maintaining.

• Gluts of any vegetable are less likely because the produce is being grown in short rows or small blocks, giving smaller amounts at a time.

• Beds can be made to almost any shape. Different materials can be used to match the style and size of the garden, and need not be expensive.

RAISED BEDS can be built at a low level or up to 1m (3ft) or table-top height.

• Cloches, protective netting and plant supports are easy to manage in a raised area.

DISADVANTAGES OF A RAISED BED

• The initial time, expense, effort and skill needed to build them especially if you are paying someone to do the work.

• They dry out more quickly than open-ground beds, requiring watering in dry weather and mulching to prevent evaporation.

• Once in place, they cannot be moved easily.

• Significantly, there are plenty of hiding places in the sides for potential pests, like slugs and snails.

Choosing the size and shape

Ideally beds should be no wider than 1.2m (4ft) so that they can be comfortably worked from both sides. If the bed is being positioned against a wall or fence, make it 60cm (24in) wide. The maximum convenient length for a bed is probably 3m (10ft); any longer can be irritatingly long to walk around. Square or rectangular beds make the best use of a small space and are easier to construct.

Deciding on materials

You can buy ready-made raised beds (wooden or recycled plastic), which have the great advantage of being easy and quick to construct and are ideal if you want only one small bed. However, doing it yourself is cheaper and gives you design flexibility. The sides are most commonly made of wood, but can be in other materials such as stone blocks. Ideally the wood is untreated to avoid any chance of chemicals leaking into the soil and the crops absorbing them. Hardwood, such as cedar or oak, lasts up to 20 years; softwood, such as pine, lasts about five years but is much less expensive.

Building the Harlow Carr beds

The 15 x 2.5cm (6 x 1in) planks for the sides are held together and kept in place by 5cm (2in) square stakes, 30cm (12in) long. Stakes with a ready-made pointed end can be ordered from timber merchants. Longer beds will need extra staking along the sides to prevent the weight of soil bending the planks; the 3m (10ft) long side of the L-shaped beds at Harlow Carr are staked halfway along. When a bed is sited on a patio, use corner brackets that are the same depth as the planks, and just stand the bed in place. Use screws rather than nails to hold everything together, since they give a more secure hold.

The wood was cut to the correct length. Timber for two of the sides of each bed had to be 5cm (2in) shorter than the two other sides to allow for the width of the timber they would butt up to. The sides of the beds were then screwed together onto the stakes to make the frame. Pre-drilled holes prevented the wood from splitting.

Once the frame was placed on the soil, it was hammered into the ground. An old piece of wood was

MAKING A RAISED BED

1 ASSEMBLE THE FRAME of the raised bed by attaching the wooden plank edges to the stakes using galvanized screws.

2 HAMMER THE CORNER STAKES of the frame into the ground with a mallet. Use an old piece of wood to protect the frame.

3 FORK OVER THE GROUND in the bottom of the raised bed before filling it. This will help drainage.

THE 3M X 3M (10FT X 10FT) PLOT AT RHS GARDEN HARLOW CARR

peas			broad beans	broad beans
beetroot & lettuce		red cabbage		
path 60cm			leeks	kale
perpetual spinach	true spinach			
			carrots & spring onion	carrots & spring onion
salad leaves & beetroot				

1.2m — 1.2m (left side), 3m (top)

EARLY CROPS

dwarf French beans	peas	climbing French beans	broad beans	broad beans
beetroot & lettuce	courgette	red cabbage	squash	sweetcorn
			leeks	kale
perpetual spinach	true spinach		chives & herbs	chives & herbs
tomato & herbs	salad leaves & beetroot		carrots & spring onion	carrots & spring onion

3m (right side)

SECOND CROPS ADDED

used to absorb the blows and prevent damage to the frame. Each corner was tapped into the soil just a few centimetres at a time to avoid twisting the frame as the stakes went in. You can hammer the stakes into the ground first and then screw the planks to them, but this can be difficult because you'd be working in an awkward position when screwing the sides to the stakes.

To prevent weeds from growing on the paths, a permeable ground-cover fabric was pinned to the soil using metal staples, then covered with a layer of ornamental bark at least 5cm (2in) deep. This makes the bed accessible even in bad weather.

Compost for filling raised beds

Having built or assembled the raised bed, the next step is to fill it with compost. It is more practical to fill it with soil fortified with organic matter. If the bed is being placed directly onto soil, the area needs to be forked over to ensure good drainage. Then spade in the compost, which must be free draining and open textured. Usually to keep the cost down, and to be

DESIGNING RAISED BEDS

If you are making more than one raised bed, sketch out plans on graph paper to scale to ensure that they fit the site. This will also help when ordering the materials as it will give you a clear idea of the quantities and sizes of the materials you need. Then mark out the area for the raised beds in the garden itself with canes and string to check that your calculations are correct and that you are happy with the plan.

HIGH YIELDS AND QUICK CROPS

Choose high-yielding varieties and fast-growing crops, such as lettuces, radishes, oriental vegetables and baby carrots, to provide several harvests each season. With some crops, such as lettuces, that means you will need to sow replacement plants in small pots before the first crop has been picked. That way, the next crop is ready to be planted the moment a gap appears in the bed.

practical, the best thing to do here is to scoop soil from the path to fill the beds, and add extra soil and compost as required.

Deciding what to grow

It is easy to get carried away when looking through seed and plant catalogues, so make sure you grow only what you really like, keeping experiments to a minimum. Ignore anything too big for your space, such as perennial vegetables like artichokes and asparagus, or that needs elaborate preparation and cultivation (such as celery), making it unsuitable for smaller areas. Remember cabbages are slow to mature and take up precious space all season. First, consider dwarf varieties and bush forms rather than rambling crops. Make the most of walls and fences for growing climbers, such as beans and peas, or provide free-standing supports made from canes wired together.

Also try growing vegetables and herbs that are ornamental as well as edible. Many lettuce and salad leaves come in red, green and purple, while basil can be dark red, and carrots have attractive, feathery foliage. Vegetables certainly don't have to be dull.

Main crops for the early part of the year

- **Broad beans**
- **Spring cabbages (for spring greens and larger cabbages)**
- **Carrots**
- **Kale (for baby leaves and to grow into winter)**
- **Leeks**
- **Peas**
- **Perpetual spinach (to provide leaves into summer, without bolting)**
- **True spinach (cool-season crop)**
- **Beetroot, lettuces and spring onions.**

All except carrots, beetroots, some of the salads and spring onions, can be started in root trainers, modules or containers under glass (though you can raise beetroot and salad in containers if you wish). They must be 'hardened off' by gradually acclimatizing them to outdoor temperatures before they are ready for planting out.

ABOVE LEFT: BEETROOTS can be sown directly into the ground in early spring and are ready to harvest as soon as they are big enough to handle.

LEFT: BROAD BEANS are so easy and can be sown the previous autumn for a really early crop.

The second main group of crops

This consists of vegetables that can't tolerate frost. At Harlow Carr, frost is a danger in late spring and even early summer. All these crops must be started under glass because, if they had been sown directly into the soil, the likes of sweetcorn, tomatoes and squashes are not likely to have a long enough growing season to mature in northern districts before autumn comes along.

- **Dwarf French beans – 'Cupidon'**

- **Climbing French beans – 'Borlotti' (for fresh pods and dried beans)**

- **Courgettes**

- **Squashes (for winter storage)**

- **Sweetcorn**

- **Tomatoes**

- **Chives and other herbs (for permanent planting)**

Around these large crops, which take up space for a relatively long period, faster-growing crops can be sown. They can be planted at the same time, or as soon as space becomes free. They include the varieties below, which were grown at Harlow Carr:

- **Beetroot – 'Chioggia Pink' (for stripy roots), 'Burpees Golden', or 'Boltardy'**

- **Cabbages – 'Kalibor' (a red, ornamental variety, for baby leaves and cabbages)**

- **Broad beans – 'Crimson Flowered' (a dwarf, ornamental variety)**

- **Carrots – 'Amini' (for young, tender roots)**

- **Courgettes – 'Venus' (a spineless, compact bush variety with green fruit)**

- **Edible flowers – borage, calendula, nasturtium, viola**

- **Florence Fennel – (the leaves can also be used for flavouring)**

EDIBLE HERBS and flowers can slot into the smallest spaces for the table or just add a bit of colour.

- **Kale – 'Redbor' (winter crop and baby leaves for summer or autumn cropping)**

- **Kohl rabi – 'Blue Delicacy' (a fast maturing, ornamental variety, good in salads)**

- **Leeks, pencil and blue-leaved varieties – 'Apollo' (highly ornamental)**

- **Onions – 'Paris Silverskin'**

- **Spring onions – 'North Holland Bloodred Redmate'**

- **Oriental vegetables (fast maturing, excellent for salads and stir fries)**

- **Peas – 'Waverex' (a dwarf, early, petit pois variety, and a heavy cropper)**

- **Perpetual spinach – 'Tirza'**

- **Tomatoes – 'Tumbler' (a compact bush variety with small red sweet tomatoes)**

- **Radishes – 'Easter Egg', 'Old Gold'**

- **Mixed salad leaves and lettuces – 'Cocarde', 'Little Gem', 'Crisp Mint'**

The Harlow Carr vegetable plot

The main criteria are growing as much as possible for as long as possible, supplying greens, carrots, courgettes, beans and peas, salads, herbs, and a few beetroots and seasonal or special vegetables.

Making a container garden

Don't worry if you only have room for assorted pots, tubs and window boxes, because you can still grow a range of produce from herbs to salads and tomatoes. In fact some varieties of tomato have been bred as compact bushes specifically for pots. To make an attractive feature, arrange the containers in groups near the kitchen.

Types of container

A huge range of shapes and materials are now readily available, the most popular being plastic, terracotta, metal and wood. All have different characteristics, advantages and disadvantages.

Clay and terracotta look very attractive, but tend to dry out more quickly than plastic, and need more regular watering. To combat this, line the inside walls with thin plastic to reduce moisture loss. Look for frost-proof rather than frost-resistant pots unless protection can be given over winter. Standing pots on 'feet' avoids water logging and therefore reduces the chance of frost damage.

Plastic pots are lighter than clay (an important consideration when you are moving pots about), dry out less easily, don't break and aren't affected by frost. Imitation terracotta pots that look just like the real thing are now available.

HERB POTS can be stuffed full of your favourite kitchen herbs like basil, coriander, mint, parsley and thyme.

Metal containers have a smart, modern look. They are frost-proof, can be heavy or lightweight, and won't dry out like clay. Their main potential problem is that they heat up (and conduct the cold) quickly.

Wooden planters, such as Versailles tubs, have a limited lifespan because the wood will rot, though this can be slowed down by lining the inside with plastic sheeting with drainage holes in the bottom.

Other possibilities include pots made of recycled materials. Almost anything can be used as a container, from old kettles, large tins and wooden boxes to buckets and wooden crates (lined with pierced plastic), depending on the look you want. Piled up old tyres can be effective, with soil poured in the centre. You can also buy growbags, from garden centres, which can be planted directly with vegetables such as tomatoes, peppers, aubergines or courgettes.

Vegetables in containers: the key points

Size Ensure that the pot size is appropriate for what you want to grow. Root vegetables such as carrots need deep pots, while beetroot sits near to the top of the soil so needs less depth. Shallower pots are also fine for salads. Big plants such as tomatoes and

---

REGIONAL RECIPE POTS

Try planting up pots with the ingredients from a particular country, or for a specific kind of recipe.

• Italian – plum tomatoes, basil, chard, sweet peppers and flat-leafed parsley.

• Greek – aubergines, tomatoes and Greek basil.

• Indian – chillies, tomatoes and coriander.

• French – tarragon, peppers and tomatoes.

---

courgettes need large pots to accommodate their roots. For tall plants that need a stable base, use a heavy pot and fill with soil-based compost.

Drainage Few vegetables thrive in waterlogged compost. Good drainage is important. Check that there are enough drainage holes in the base of the container. If there is only one, drill more. Sticking masking tape over the area to be drilled prevents cracking. Cover the base of the pot with old crocks or stones to help with drainage, and raise the pots on feet to let the water drain. It is important to use a lightish, free-draining compost with added grit. If you're using growbags, make a few holes in the bottom, or snip two of the corners off to make small holes to allow the excess water to drain away. For new potatoes, use polythene bags or old compost sacks. Make drainage holes in the bottom, fill up to one-third with potting compost, plant a couple of tubers, and cover with more compost as the foliage appears.

Watering Potting compost needs to be moist at all times. Do not rely on rainfall because it may not penetrate the leaf cover of the plants, or be heavy enough to soak down to the roots. If it is allowed to dry out, it is often difficult to re-wet and your crops will suffer as a consequence. To make the job easier, you can mix non-organic water-retaining gel or powder in with the compost when planting. The gel swells when wetted, and then releases water gradually back into the compost. Mulching the surface with gravel or other decorative materials looks good and helps minimize evaporation. If you have many pots, it might be worth installing an automatic irrigation system. To check if a plant needs a drink, scrape away the surface or mulch to see how moist the compost is. Large containers take longer to dry out than smaller ones.

Potting compost Use either a water-retentive peat- or bark-based potting compost, or a soil- or loam-based medium for your vegetables. A good-quality compost can make a lot of difference. There are plenty of alternatives to peat now available. John Innes potting composts are soil based, and are all suitable for vegetable containers. Most types of multi-purpose potting composts are also suitable.

Feeding The relatively small amount of compost in a pot will have limited nutrients for plants and, if the plant is frequently watered, the nutrients may

quickly be flushed out. Incorporating a controlled-release fertilizer on planting will help; otherwise use a general-purpose feed. For fruiting crops such as tomatoes, use a high-potash feed once the fruit begins to form. A general fertilizer has nitrogen (N), phosphorous (P) and potassium (K) in equal proportions. Nitrogen-rich fertilizers encourage leafy growth so are good for leaf crops like spinach, chard, and lettuce. Phosphorous-rich fertilizers encourage root growth so are good for root crops. Potassium-rich fertilizers encourage fruit and flower formation and are good for fruiting crops such as tomatoes and courgettes. In practice, any balanced liquid feed is satisfactory.

Position The advantage of pots is that they can be moved in or out of the sun as required, especially if they're on a base with wheels. In general, though, they are too heavy to keep shifting about, so choose your position with care. Avoid windy areas when growing climbers, and remember that an open, windy site can dry out a pot as quickly as one in hot sun – but vegetables dislike shade.

CONTAINERS are also very useful when it comes to sowing seeds of early crops indoors, for later planting out.

Know your plot

Soil is the raw material of vegetable growing. It is teeming with harmless and beneficial bacteria, fungi and other mini-creatures that recycle organic matter and use air, water and minerals to make plant food. The soil can hold enough water and sufficient plant food to sustain many weeks' growth. Best of all, it needs only a little input from the gardener.

Taking a look at the soil

Before you decide what you want to grow in it, you need to know a little bit about your patch of soil.

Dig a narrow, sharp-sided pit about 60cm (24in) deep, and check the colour of the sides. There should be a dark topsoil layer at least 20cm (8in) deep above a paler subsoil. The topsoil should be open and friable, ideally with plant roots visible to their full depth. Hard, compacted soils block growing roots and drainage, so careful cultivation is required to open up the soil.

Subsoils might be hard clay, or bedrock, possibly coarse, stony material, or even deep sand. There is not much you can do about them, but at least you can be aware of the degree of drainage they offer and what potential there is for plant roots to grow.

If you have solid subsoil, think about making a raised bed to increase the drainage and depth of good soil. The advantage of a porous subsoil is that it allows the plant roots to explore for nutrients and for water during periods of dry weather.

IS YOUR SOIL ACID OR ALKALINE?

Measuring the pH of your soil enables you to determine whether the soil is acid or alkaline. A pH of 7 is neutral, less than 7 is acid and more than 7 is alkaline. Vegetables grow best in a slightly acid soil with a pH of 6.5, although pH 7–7.5 helps reduce club root disease in the cabbage family.

Although a laboratory test is best (and not hugely expensive), soil test kits are available from all good gardening stores. A test kit can quickly give you an indication of your soil's pH, using a simple colour system to show the pH level. Acid soil usually turns the testing solution an orange-yellow colour, neutral turns it green and alkaline turns it a dark green. If the soil is acid, spread garden lime (finely ground chalk or limestone) and mix it into the soil in the amounts the test results suggest are needed to raise the pH.

TESTING THE pH OF YOUR SOIL USING A KIT

1 PUT A SMALL SAMPLE of your soil into the pH testing kit test tube.

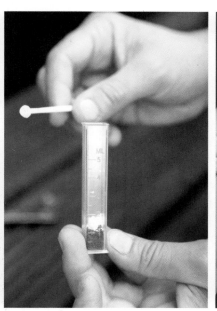

2 FOLLOW THE INSTRUCTIONS carefully by adding testing chemicals to your sample.

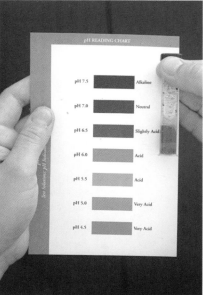

3 COMPARE THE COLOUR of the resulting mixture with those on the supplied colour chart. The best match indicates your soil's pH.

Checking the drainage

Once you have examined your pit, fill it with water, cover, and leave overnight. If the water is still there the next day, drainage is poor and raised beds or a drainage system might be needed. Excess water excludes air from the soil and roots can't survive long without air. In effect, the plants drown.

Identifying the elements

Roll some of the topsoil between your hands. If it flakes and crumbles, it is low in clay. If it feels gritty between finger and thumb, it is sandy. A soapy or silky feel suggests silt. And if it is easy to roll into a sausage shape, it is clay.

Soil structure

When growing vegetables, the better the soil structure, the better the crop. Soils consist of minerals, clay, sand and silt, which are coated in and bound by organic materials to produce small lumps called peds. These lumps give structure to the soil and

prevent it from becoming a solid mass impenetrable to roots.

Peds have air spaces between them which allow oxygen, water and roots to enter the soil. The roots then extract water and nutrients from the peds. Working or trampling on your soil, especially when it is wet – builders are common culprits! – ruins the peds. On the other hand, digging in well-rotted organic matter, such as garden compost or manure, applying mulches of organic matter, and working your soil only when it is reasonably dry, preserves and enhances the soil structure.

Adding well-rotted organic matter – and indeed good gardening generally – is good for garden wildlife. It boosts the number of soil organisms, and they in turn feed larger ones, including insects and worms, which eventually feed the likes of hedgehogs, slow worms and birds. Ideally, aim to add at least one bucketful of organic matter every square metre (or yard) every two

---

CLAY

Clay is rich in nutrients, it drains poorly in winter and is slow to warm up in spring. But it is usually moist in summer, and can grow good crops of most vegetables (see Improving Your Soil, page 28).

SANDY SOIL

Sandy soil drains easily in winter and warms up quickly in spring, but holds few nutrients and dries out in summer. It is good for early crops, but later ones often need watering.

LOAM

In between clay and sand comes the crumbly soil, loam. It combines most of the best features of clay and sand, but is all too rare.

SILT

Silt behaves like loam but is easily smeared and damaged in winter. It is very fertile but rarely encountered in gardens.

DIG IN well-rotted organic matter when the soil is reasonably dry to preserve and enhance your soil's structure.

or three years. Adding well-rotted organic matter is good for all soil types, whether you have clay, sand or silt. It improves the soil structure, makes clay soils more free-draining and sandy soils more water-retentive.

The weather's effects

Wind and frost

Even the best soil is no good if it is in the wrong place. Your crops will need as much sun as possible, and few are worth growing where buildings or trees limit the summer sun to less than six hours a day.

Windy conditions also slow vegetable growth and make cloches and horticultural fleece hard to keep in place. Hedges make good windbreaks, being cost effective and good for wildlife; fences are an alternative in small gardens and where quick results are wanted. Porous fences (with 50 percent gaps) and deciduous hedges are best because they slow the wind, rather than solid barriers that force the wind up, over and down, creating a buffeting effect.

Frosts can be damaging and are worst in low-lying sites where cold air collects. Because cold air is heavy,

POLYTUNNELS, greenhouses, cloches and fleece are all ways to protect your crops from wind and frost, but they too are best in sheltered locations, away from frost pockets.

gardens at the foot of a hill, or where walls and hedges prevent the cold air from draining away to lower levels, are likely to suffer the worst frosts. Nearby high trees and buildings are also sources of cold air because they leak heat into the night sky, chilling the air which then sinks to the ground.

WILDLIFE

A garden can be an oasis for wildlife in built-up areas. If there are canals, railways and parks nearby, an even wider range of wildlife can benefit from the shelter and food it provides. Compost bins, thick organic mulches, watering in summer evenings to leave the soil moist for hours, leaving plants to go to seed and using green 'manure' crops (see page 29) that cover the ground over winter, all help.

Some wildlife needs to be kept away. Pigeons, for example, devour salad seedlings, but most wildlife is an asset to a vegetable plot. Robins won't seriously deplete your worm population, hedgehogs eat pests, and foxes take mice.

THE CHAFFINCH is a common garden nest-builder.

RAISED BEDS provide crops with a deep fertile soil and are ideal on poorly-drained sites.

The last frost in late spring marks the beginning of the growing season, and the growing season ends – except for some hardy plants – with the first frosts in early autumn. The longer the growing season the better, especially for frost-sensitive plants such as pumpkins and sweetcorn. Gardens in frost pockets experience a much shorter growing season than gardens where cold air can drain away.

In general, inland and upland areas are colder than coastal regions, and urban areas are usually warmer than the countryside since the warm masonry and paving emits heat at night. Conditions are obviously cooler as you move away from the equator. The growing season gets shorter the further you go, and eventually crops such as squashes and tomatoes cannot be grown outdoors.

Wet winters, dry summers

Wet winters make harvesting and preparing the soil difficult, and can spoil the produce even if there is good drainage. While gardeners in wet districts can stand on planks so that they don't damage the soil, a good alternative is to build raised beds that drain well, warm up earlier in spring and can be worked from paths. But winter rains are not all bad: they fill

MULCHING adds a layer of organic matter to the soil surface, which helps to reduce evaporation from the soil.

the soil with water until it can take no more (usually around midwinter). The surplus then drains away, but the stored rain is available for plants during early summer.

Dry summers can greatly reduce the quantity and quality of crops. Raised beds help gardeners in areas prone to summer droughts because the greater depth of fertile soil gives plant roots more to explore for water. Adding organic matter, by mulching or digging in, and avoiding compacted soils allows the equivalent of 5cm (2in) of rain to be stored in the soil – enough to keep plants going for two weeks.

PROTECTING TENDER PLANTS

FLEECE TENTS or tunnels offer quick frost protection for tender seedlings prone to late spring frosts.

MINI POLYTUNNELS made from clear plastic sheeting over hoops are a cost-effective way of extending the season.

Preparing the plot

The preparations depend on what kind of plot you're hoping to create. If you want the maximum amount of fresh produce from a small space, consider raised beds. You'll need easy access to compost bins, tools and fertilizers. But if the plot is part of an ornamental garden, consider decorative paths and bed edging, and hiding the less attractive elements behind a trellis.

DECORATIVE TOUCHES, like woven edging (left), make the difference between an ornamental and a working vegetable garden (above).

Relaxed garden or formal layout?

Unless you are developing an already established plot, you will need to plan the shape, size and look of your vegetable garden, and decide where it should be positioned to best suit your requirements. Everything will depend on what you want out of the feature: is it to be a practical area designed to produce as much as possible for the kitchen (see pages 16 and 35)? Or is it to be primarily decorative? Should it be sympathetic in style with the rest of the garden? Or is it an isolated feature that complements other areas or stands happily alone?

Traditionally, a vegetable garden has neat, well-tended rows of crops set in bare, well-tilled, weed-free soil. In an informal setting, try scattered patches of crops among showy plants, with wigwams of peas and beans dotted here and there, and pumpkins scrambling over compost bins and even hedges. In geometric gardens, a formal potager with neatly edged beds might be better, perhaps with single, individual (or 'dot-planted') tomatoes and obelisks of climbing beans in a carpet of salads or a regimented block of red cabbages or beetroot.

Positioning your plot

Place a vegetable plot adjacent to a sunny wall or fence; they are ideal as supports for climbing vegetables, but remember that soil in the rain shadow of walls and fences can be dry, so aim to have beds at least 60cm (24in) wide along fences and walls, and manure them generously so that they retain moisture well. Hedges rob adjacent soil of moisture and nutrients, so make sure that the beds are fed and watered well. Also, ideally have a 60cm (24in) path between hedge and plot.

Tackling the weeds

You'll need to dig the vegetable garden to remove weeds and debris, and to incorporate fertilizers, compost and possibly lime to reduce acidity. Preliminary cultivation is worthwhile, even if you intend to follow a no-digging regime later. There is some evidence that avoiding digging leads to a healthier, more productive soil and, for many gardeners who do not relish heavy digging, it is the only practical way to cultivate clay soil. Rotavating a weedy soil to clear it is not a good idea, since the machine chops up the weed roots into many pieces –

all of which then take root and regrow. It is best to remove weeds either by hand, or by treating with weedkiller (see page 43). Weedkillers containing glyphosate are the most environmentally friendly, since the active chemical does not remain active in the soil after they have done their work. Perennial weeds such as bindweed, dock and dandelion, thistles, couch grass and nettles, need to be dug out by hand or treated with weedkiller. Annual weeds such as groundsel, chickweed and fat hen are best hoed off as they emerge – before they can set seed. Don't add perennial weeds to the compost; instead lay them out exposed to sun where they will soon dry out and die.

Improving your soil

Fertile conditions boost the size, flavour, yield and quality of your vegetables. If you can, add bulky, well-rotted organic matter, such as garden or municipal compost or farmyard manure, every second or third year to half or one-third of your plot. Some crops, such as carrots and parsnips, are best grown on soil that was manured the previous year. As a rough guide, one bucketful of well-rotted material to every square metre (or yard) is enough, but double this amount could be used for thin, poor soil and for greedy crops.

Bulky manures are not enough on their own. Greedy crops, such as brassicas, beetroot, spinach and celery, need the boost of a general fertilizer containing roughly equal amounts of nitrogen, phosphorus and potassium. They like about 140g (5oz) per square metre (or yard) of a fertilizer containing 7 percent of each nutrient. Leeks, onions, French and runner beans need 100g (3.5oz), and everything else benefits from 70g (2.5oz). Carrots and peas don't usually need feeding.

Use other fertilizers according to their nitrogen content (the packet should give details). So, for a 3 percent nitrogen fertilizer, you would use slightly more than twice as much per square metre (or yard). However, be aware that some fertilizers do not contain potassium and should not be used on certain soils, for example sandy ones, that are low in potassium.

MANY CROPS really benefit from extra feeding. Organic and inorganic fertilizers are available.

TOOLS

Having the right tools for the job, and plenty of them, makes vegetable growing much easier and leaves more time for you to enjoy the end result. Good inexpensive tools are sold by DIY or garden stores and are widely available second hand. Make sure you clean your tools and store them carefully after every use. That way they will last longer and be a pleasure to use every time. A typical starter-kit for growing your own vegetables includes:

- a spade and fork
- a rake
- a pair of secateurs
- a hose pipe
- a push or draw hoe
- a watering can
- a trowel and hand fork
- boots and gloves.

GREEN MANURES

Crops can be grown just to improve the soil. Grown in autumn or over winter, when the ground is otherwise bare, they stop the nutrients from being washed out by rain. When dug in during autumn green manures are also ideal for clay soil, which can compact further over winter.

Sow mustard or fodder radish in late summer as the main crops are being harvested and removed. Vetches or tares and rye can be sown in early autumn and allowed to grow over winter, before being dug in during early spring at least two weeks before sowing the next year's crops.

These green manures won't add much to the soil but they do save nutrients, reduce potential pollution and make the soil more workable.

A GREEN MANURE CROP also keeps weeds at bay and makes an excellent addition to the compost heap.

Managing the compost

Composting can be one of the most rewarding gardening activities, and is good for the environment as well as garden wildlife. In essence, it is just gathering organic waste and allowing natural organisms, widespread in the environment, to break down the waste to a brown mass of soil conditioner.

Use two compost bins: one to fill up while the other is rotting down. When you have emptied one, tip the contents of the second into the first bin as a way of turning the heap. If space is short, use small bins, but try to avoid those with a capacity of less than 1cu m (1.3cu yd). Stand them on previously dug-over soil or, if this is not possible, spread a bucketful of soil under the bin. You can even dig a small pit beneath the bin to increase its capacity.

Add a mix of organic waste from the garden and kitchen to the bin. About a third of the waste should be soft green nitrogen-rich material such as kitchen waste and lawn mowings; the rest should be straw-like or woody carbon-rich material, such as spent crops. Keep adding waste until the bin is full, adding water if the contents look dry. Then leave them to rot.

Turn the heap with a fork, once or twice a year. Mix in air and add water, more green waste or more carbon-rich waste as required to speed up the rotting process and improve quality. Realistically, garden compost cannot rival the manufactured material. This is made with large volumes of waste that's mechanically mixed and chopped and composted at a high temperature to produce a fine, peat-like result. Garden compost will usually be a bit twiggy and rough, but any unrotted material can be added to the next bin, and the remainder will be an effective soil improver. Perennial weeds should not be added to the mix, since they will simply grow there, unless thoroughly killed by desiccation first.

In small gardens, worm composting in 'wormeries' might be a better bet. Bins can be quite small, and take little waste. Worm bins consist of an upper chamber where the waste is added, and a lower sump where liquid collects. The liquid contains plant nutrients and is watered onto growing crops. Eventually the upper chamber fills with compost, and that's added to the garden. The worms are recovered for the next batch. Both bins and worms can be bought as kits from specialist suppliers.

All about growing

Raising strong and healthy seedlings is a critical part of growing your own veg, whether you are germinating your own seed or buying in seedlings as plug plants that have already been started off by a nursery. All good crops depend on a good start, after all. Seed can either be sown directly where it is to grow or sown in pots or trays and then planted out later.

Where to start

When planning your crops, you need to decide whether you are going to grow from seed or from plug plants bought from a specialist supplier, from a local nursery or by mail order. The range of plants available – and of sources – is growing all the time. There are pros and cons to seed sowing as well as using plug plants: you will have to weigh up what suits you and your garden's conditions.

Perennial crops can be grown from seed, but it's a lot less effort to buy young plants. Potatoes are not grown from seed but from 'seed potatoes', and alliums, except leeks, are usually grown from 'sets' or bulbs. If you want to grow from seed, there are two ways: either in trays or containers for later transplanting, or by sowing direct into drills made in the soil. Which method you choose depends on the crop as well as the growing conditions. You might, for example, choose to sow in trays because you have problems with hungry mice or birds, and the young plants need some growth before they are exposed.

Germinating your seeds

Seed germination is related to temperature. Carrots sown in cold soil in late winter for harvesting in early summer might take 21 days or more to germinate, but if they're sown in mid-spring for a summer crop, they should come up in 14 days.

SEEDLINGS

Small seed makes small seedlings, and these take a long time to put on good growth (carrots and onions are good examples) whereas large seed (e.g. peas and broad beans) produce large seedlings that get off to a flying start.

However, plants from warm countries need about 12°C (53°F) to germinate well, and that's why tomatoes, peppers and aubergines – all grown from small seed – are sown indoors in early spring. They'll start growing quickly, and have a growing season that's long enough to produce a good crop before the autumn frosts. Large-seeded runner and French beans, sweetcorn, courgettes, marrows, pumpkins and squashes can be sown outdoors in late spring and early summer and, being large-seeded, grow fast and have enough time to crop well in southern areas. Indoor sowing is necessary in other regions.

Seedlings are vulnerable to fungal diseases such as damping off. Fungicidal seed dressings are no longer available to gardeners, but avoiding disease by sowing at the optimum time, when the soil is warm and not too wet, greatly reduces risk of disease. Watering seedlings raised indoors with copper-based fungicides also protects them.

THE SMALL SIZE of seedlings means that many can be sown closely together, but they will soon need potting on if they are to flourish.

However, disease can often be avoided altogether by using clean containers and clean water.

Sowing direct in the soil outdoors is quick and easy, and the seedlings look after themselves, developing strong root systems that resist drought and disease. The downside is that they are vulnerable to pests, diseases and the weather, and to competition for space and food from weeds.

DIRECT-SOWING is where seeds are sown where they are to grow in straight drills in the soil.

Soil temperatures of at least 6°C (43°F) are needed for most seed to germinate, and this is reached by mid-spring in most of England, two weeks later in colder districts and two weeks earlier in mild regions. Slow-germinating seed includes parsnips, carrots and onions which take, on average, 14–21 days to emerge; members of the cabbage family and lettuces may take just seven days, and most other seed takes somewhere in between.

Sowing seeds outdoors

Seed must be buried in the soil, but not so deeply that it cannot emerge, and not so shallowly that it dries out unless watered or rained on. To create the right conditions, you need a seedbed in which the previously cultivated soil is raked level to create a smooth layer of finely divided soil over firm, but not too hard, underlying soil. This can be done only if the soil is dry. Spread a light dressing of an all-purpose fertilizer on the soil before raking to ensure that the emerging seedlings aren't short of nutrients.

Make a groove, called a drill, in the surface just deep enough to cover the seed to about twice its diameter or, in the case of small seed, as shallow as possible but still enough to cover. The large seed of peas, beans and sweetcorn need a drill about 5cm (2in) deep, the moderate-sized seed of the cabbage family, spinach and beetroot need a 2.5cm (1in) drill, and the fine seed of onions, carrots, parsnips and lettuces, a drill no more than 2cm (¾in) deep.

The groove can be made using the corner of a hoe or rake or, better for small seed, by using the length of a broom handle pressed into the soil. Water the drill and place the seed in it in a sparse, continuous flow, with about 1cm (½in) between each onion and carrot seed, for example. Alternatively, sow five or six seeds wherever you want a plant (e.g. lettuces or turnips), later thinning to one plant. Then draw back the soil with the hoe or rake to fill the drill.

The seed and soil must be in close contact if the seed is to take up moisture from the ground. The easiest way to make sure this happens is to firm down the soil by pressing on it with the head of the rake. Do it firmly if the soil is dry, and lightly if it's moist. Some soils pack down under rain so solidly that the seed cannot emerge; if this is a danger in your veg plot, cover the seed instead with fine potting compost.

Transplanting from the seedbeds

Young vegetables can be carefully dug out of seedbeds and replanted in a fresh spot. This is the traditional way of raising leeks and members of the cabbage family. They are set at the same depth as in the seedbed or, in the case of the cabbages, are buried up to the depth of the lowest leaves.

NURSERY BEDS are sometimes used to bring plants on before they are finally planted out. Keep them well watered.

SOW FAST-GROWING CROPS into all available gaps to increase the productivity of your plot.

Watering before and after transplanting limits the shock. 'Puddling in' ensures a quick recovery and good subsequent growth. Most plants are best transplanted as soon as you can handle them, but leave cabbages until they have five true leaves, and leeks until they are pencil thick. Trimming leaves and roots makes the plants easier to handle but slows recovery, and is best avoided.

Sowing in containers

Raising plants in pots and cell trays involves more work and expense than sowing direct in the ground, but it saves seed since you just sow one or just a few per pot. Excess seedlings of expensive seed, e.g. hybrid Brussels sprouts and leeks, can be transferred as young seedlings to another pot or bed to avoid wastage. Using trays or pots leads to a higher success rate than sowing in the ground where there is more risk of diseases, pests and weather damage. There is little choice with some crops like tomatoes and peppers: these need to be germinated under cover before it is warm enough for planting out.

Vegetable seed is undemanding, and any good proprietary seed or multipurpose compost – peat-based or peat-free – is suitable. Don't use home-made composts because they are liable to contain pests, diseases and harmful nutrient levels.

Time to plant out

Once the root system binds the compost together, seedlings can be planted out. Don't delay and wait until the plants are big and start to go yellow, but remember that tender crops like courgettes and tomatoes must not be planted out until the risk of frost has passed. To be sure, wait until early summer with these – or later, if you are in a cold area. Again, 'puddling in' (see page 70) is very helpful.

Repeated sowings

Some plants, e.g. Brussels sprouts, runner beans and tomatoes, crop continuously while others, such as potatoes and carrots, can be stored. But repeated sowings at intervals, called 'successional sowing', is necessary for a continuous supply of other crops, such as peas, beans, lettuces and cauliflowers. If you sow no more than you are likely to need over a two-week period each time, and then start again when the first plants are about 5–8cm (2–3¼in) high, you will avoid waste and seldom be without produce.

PLUG PLANTS raised by yourself or a specialist supplier should be planted as soon as they are large enough and the weather permits.

INTERPLANTING quick crops, as here with radish (black Spanish) 'Montana' in between sweetcorn, is a good way to make the most of any spare space among vegetables which take longer to mature.

Intercropping and catch cropping

Some plants grow slowly but eventually become large, and you can use the space between the growing vegetables for one more quick crop before the larger vegetables block out the sun. For example, peas sown in mid-spring need 60cm (24in) of space each side so that the pods can be gathered, but they won't cast much shade until early summer. In the meantime lettuces, spinach and rocket can be grown near the peas, which is known as 'intercropping'.

Where a crop is gathered early, or planted late, there are opportunities to grow crops before and after. This is called 'catch cropping'. So, broad beans sown in late winter can be cleared away in midsummer, leaving time for a row of French beans (in southern areas) to be sown for use in the autumn. Leeks planted out in midsummer leave time for a row of lettuces to be planted in early spring and gathered before the leeks need setting out.

ROTATION OF CROPS

Growing each crop on a different piece of land by rotating them each year can help reduce the effect of soil pests and diseases. (Airborne pests and diseases can travel miles, and can't be controlled in this way.) Where possible, aim for a three-year rotation. Divide the vegetable plot into equal sections and choose which crops you want to grow. Group them by plant family (by pests and diseases), then soil requirements and soil benefits. For example, grow potatoes and tomatoes on a specific area (after manuring) in year one; peas, broad beans, carrots, parsnips, onions, shallots, leeks and garlic in year two; and in year three (after adding lime if necessary), the cabbage family. Other crops suffer fewer soil problems, and can be grown wherever is convenient.

Extending the season

All vegetable gardeners are in the habit of extending the season of their crops by raising seedlings on a sunny windowsill; it gives plants a head start while it is cold outside. Even so, not much can be gathered from the garden until midsummer. To really extend the season you will need some extra tricks, such as warming the soil in spring or using a glasshouse.

AN UNHEATED PROPAGATOR acts like a mini-greenhouse and is perfect for germinating seeds of tender vegetables.

Sowing in the warmth

Most crops can be started off early in a greenhouse or indoors. Greenhouses can also be used to extend the season well into autumn for crops that respond well to a long season, such as tomatoes and aubergines, since they offer that extra warmth. A sunny windowsill can be used to raise young plants, particularly if you use a white board behind the plants so that they get light from both sides, and not just the front. Windows provide less light than you might think, so aim to move plants outside as soon as possible. Avoid sowing so early that seedlings have to stay on the windowsill for long periods.

Moving your plants outside

Use a mini-greenhouse or, much better, a cold frame as a halfway house to ease congestion on your windowsill and acclimatize plants to the outside world. When the plants are put out in the vegetable garden, they can be protected by being covered with fleece. This acclimatization process is called 'hardening off'. It avoids sudden changes in airflow, humidity and temperature which can lead to poor growth and, often, premature flowering.

GREENHOUSE GARDENERS enjoy a long season of growing, raising tender crops like tomatoes and melons with ease.

Warming the soil

Early crops can be sown outdoors by taking advantage of plastic materials. Covering a seedbed with polythene (use clear or black; clear gives most warmth, black suppresses weeds) for at least six weeks before sowing warms the soil enough to risk early sowings. A covering like this allows seed to be sown up to four weeks earlier than usual. For example, it's risky to sow carrot seed before early spring, but if a seedbed is prepared and covered in mid-winter, seed sown in late winter has a good chance of success.

After sowing, the polythene can be replaced by fleece. Fleece is an amazing non-woven plastic fabric that lets in light, rain and pesticide sprays, and retains some warmth. Sowings can be made under fleece about two weeks before seed can be sown in open ground, if the fleece is suspended over the soil on hoops. Beneath the fleece the plants are protected from the worst frost and flying pests, including birds. Unfortunately slugs and weeds appreciate fleece as much as crops, so you will need to keep an eye out for both. In cold weather, use a double layer of fleece, reducing it to a single layer as soon as possible.

SUNNY, SHELTERED PATIOS are almost as good as greenhouses: the bricks and paving emit heat at night as they cool down.

BELL CLOCHES are single-plant solutions for the gardener without a greenhouse.

VINE TOMATOES are ideal crops for glasshouses because they respond well to the extra warmth and longer season.

Covering with fleece for the early part of the crops' life also encourages an early harvest. When transplants are covered by fleece they can be expected to mature about two weeks before uncovered crops.

Cloches are really pint-sized greenhouses, about 50cm (20in) tall, and can be used in the same way as fleece, although they can be prone to blowing over in windy weather. Use them to cover tender plants such as aubergines, bush tomatoes, courgettes, melons and peppers, in summer. Cloches can make all the difference in northern gardens where there is no greenhouse.

Gardeners lucky enough to have a glazed porch, conservatory, or even just a picture window can grow tender plants like aubergines, peppers (especially chilli peppers) and tomatoes in pots 45cm (18in) diameter or larger, or in growbags. In fact, a sunny city balcony or patio can be a useful sun-trap nearly as good as a greenhouse for growing these tender crops.

COLD FRAME DOORS can be propped open on hot spring days and closed at night when frosts are still possible.

Coping with problems

Vegetables are just as attractive to pests and diseases as they are to people. The tender texture and mild flavours probably make crops vulnerable, but they do have in-built mechanisms for resisting pests and diseases. There are also many beneficial insects and other organisms that prey on pests or inhibit disease. Keep your plants well nourished and watered to help them to ward off attacks.

Coping with pests

You can't miss the likes of snails and slugs (easily the worst offenders in vegetable gardens), caterpillars and rabbits; other pests, such as red spider mite, are barely visible, and some are invisible without a microscope. Insects are by far the most prolific pests. They feed on plants by sucking – blackfly attack runner beans and leaf miners are often seen on beetroot and celery – or tunnelling into tubers. Insects also spread virus diseases; greenfly for example, is a carrier of potato viruses.

Helping plants to fight

Vegetable growers should boost natural counter-measures; avoid harming helpful organisms and do not wage war directly on pests and diseases. A certain level of disease and pest attack has to be tolerated, especially if the edible part of the crop is not directly affected. You can't have a completely problem-free vegetable garden even if you use pesticides, but you can still be a successful vegetable grower without using them.

The first line of defence is knowing that well-grown plants with sufficient water and nutrients fend off insect attacks much more readily than stressed plants. Second, make life inhospitable for the pests, removing hiding places and limiting access by getting rid of debris and weeds, and raking the soil level to deter slugs, for example. Third, prevent them

A WEED-FREE SOIL helps to keep problems at bay.

reaching the crop with barriers and mesh. Carrot fly and cabbage root fly can be excluded with fleece or, even better, insect-proof mesh. The carrot fly travels low down and, if forced to rise over a barrier, it cannot descend after the barrier for about 2m (6½ft). That's why you need to surround carrot crops with a 50cm (20in) high barrier of plastic sheeting. The best way to counter the cabbage root fly, which lays its eggs at the foot of brassicas, is to put a 7–15cm (2¾–6in) felt collar (see page 71) around the base of the plant. Large pests like the caterpillars of cabbage white butterflies can be removed by hand, but this can be time-consuming.

The next step is, where possible, to choose varieties that resist attack, such as fly-resistant carrots. Although mixing plants, for example onions and carrots, to confuse pests is often advocated, there is little evidence that it is effective. Similarly, plants with strong odours such as marigolds are believed to protect vegetables from pests; it may or may not work for you – but there is no harm in trying.

The final remedy is to apply an insecticide or other chemical. This should seldom be necessary, and so-called directed sprays with a physical action (such as oils, soaps and fatty acids) will do least harm to

HEDGEHOGS are known to eat slugs and snails and should be welcomed.

helpful insects. Of those that poison insects, the natural ones, such as pyrethrum and derris, are short-lived and mild. If all else fails, a synthetic insecticide such as bifenthrin (a synthetic version of pyrethrum) can be tried. It will persist for longer than many natural materials and is potentially harmful to helpful insects, so it should be used with discretion.

Dealing with slugs and snails

These are a special case. Slug pellets give good control, but but they are not organic and some gardeners are uneasy about using them although there is no direct evidence that those containing metaldehyde harm wildlife. They must be used as the manufacturer instructs, of course, and only very sparsely – three or four pellets per plant is enough. If used too liberally, the cumulative effect and danger to pets and wildlife is much increased. In very wet weather even pellets may be ineffective. Alternatively try aluminium sulphate powder. Pellets containing ferric phosphate are compatible with organic gardening. Biological control, where nematodes (microscopic, worm-like animals) are watered onto the soil to infect slugs with a lethal bacterium is often effective in summer, but affects only certain slugs. In fact, good cultural control may be sufficient, where hiding places are eliminated and biological control is used. Other more traditional remedies like beer traps and half-grapefruit skins are worth trying if you are averse to all other methods, but they are unreliable, and you should expect to lose some of your crops.

Plant diseases

Diseases are caused by infections of bacteria, viruses, and especially fungi. Again, plants grown in good conditions are better able to fight off infection than those under stress. Where possible, choose plants that have some resistance to disease. For example, there are potatoes resistant to potato blight, peas that resist powdery mildew and certain cabbage family plants that resist clubroot (all three being fungal diseases). But you can also use fungicides to prevent fungal diseases. (There are no fungicides available to UK gardeners that can treat disease, only those that can help prevent it.) When fungal diseases are suspected, dust with sulphur (to counter powdery mildews, which occur in dry weather). Peas and the cucumber family are especially vulnerable plants. Sulphur dusts can prevent this.

A BEER TRAP can be used to attract and kill slugs.

Downy mildews strike in wet spells. Younger leaves (such as spinach) are usually unaffected, as are lettuce hearts. Fungal diseases are greatly influenced by the weather. Potato blight, for example (which also attacks tomatoes) is one of the commonest diseases, but it needs the warmth and moisture that generally occur in wet spells in late summer and early autumn. Blight can be tackled with copper-containing fungicides or mancozeb, a synthetic, protective material. In areas with high rainfall where blight is almost inevitable, regular spraying of cultivars every ten days might be necessary.

Soil-dwelling fungi

Clubroot of brassicas and onion white rot, for example, are special cases. There are no soil fungicides, and resistant cultivars are often lacking. Crop rotation (see page 35) is the first line of defence. Being confined to the soil, these diseases spread slowly. Scrupulous destruction of infected material reduces the soil spore levels and, for clubroot, liming the soil (see pages 21 and 71) will reduce the severity of the disease. Bacterial and viral diseases are seldom a problem in UK vegetable gardens. If such diseases do turn up, however, the only remedy is to discard the infected plants and start again.

Growing healthy plants

Robust vegetables are not prone to disorders, and it is in your interests to make sure that yours are well grown. They are hungry crops, and should be fed with all the nutrients they need. This can be difficult when you are gardening organically, because it takes time and energy. Organic fertilizers must be applied well in advance (they are slower-acting than artificial fertilizers) and combined with careful soil management, including manuring, composting, mulching and crop rotation. The signs of a fertile soil are a rich, dark brown crumbly top soil that contains plenty of decomposed organic matter. Even then, it will require intensive care to maintain. Chicken manure pellets or synthetic fertilizers can provide temporary relief (for one season at most) by adding nitrogen. In fact, most apparent disorders in vegetable crops result from insufficient nitrogen, which affects the rate of plant growth and the yield. If nitrogen-rich fertilizer does not help, then the problem is usually lack of water. In the longer term, the remedy for both nitrogen deficiency and lack of water is to increase the frequency with which organic composts and manures are applied; artificial fertilizers really offer only a 'quick fix'. Well-rotted compost and manures are best applied to the soil in early spring, improving the soil before most crops are planted out (see page 22).

On sandy soils in particular, yellowing between the veins can be caused by lack of magnesium. Spraying the foliage with Epsom salts – 105g (4oz) in 5ltr (8.8pts) of water – should fix this. If the problem persists, lack of water is again probably to blame.

Other disorders include water-logging and cold or frost damage.

Keeping weeds in check

Vegetables are quickly ruined if there is competition from weeds (see page 27), especially at the seedling stage. Weeds can easily take hold because vegetables are grown in widely spaced rows with areas of bare soil. Few vegetables cast enough shade to deter or block them.

Fortunately, perennial weeds are easily removed by digging and hoeing, but those with persistent rhizomes, such as couch grass, horsetail and bindweed, can be troublesome. If digging them out doesn't work, you can use a glyphosate weedkiller when they are in full growth in summer.

Annual weeds, on the other hand, can easily persist among vegetables. They do this by shedding huge numbers of seeds – 4,000 or more in the case of fat hen and groundsel plants. These seeds remain dormant, but through light and fluctuating temperatures they can 'sense' when they are near the surface and when conditions will probably result in good growth. Their ability to detect high nitrogen levels ensures that they germinate at the right time.

Old gardens and allotments usually have large numbers of dormant weed seeds in the soil. In new gardens this is much less of a problem, and if you are careful never to let weeds set seed, you will avoid a weed problem indefinitely. Hoeing, raking and hand-weeding to remove all weed seedlings amongst young crops is the first step. Keep checking that none survives to set seed, and if they appear, pull them out by hand. As weeds may well develop after being pulled up, they should be disposed of and not left lying around or added to the compost bin. Where weeds are numerous, some crops, including cucumbers, courgettes, garlic, marrows, onions, pumpkins, shallots, squashes, sweetcorn and tomatoes, can be grown through holes made in black polythene or other opaque material which covers the soil. Alternatively, thick organic mulches can be used to eliminate weeds for all but the garlic, onions and shallots.

By creating seedbeds (known as stale weedbeds) well in advance of the intended sowing or planting dates, the weeds get a chance to germinate and you can hoe them out. Few will germinate following vegetable crops.

PLANT THROUGH a black plastic mulch for low-maintenance weed control. It also warms the soil.

Planning what to grow

Since you can't grow everything you want in a small vegetable plot, stick to your favourite vegetables and those in which freshness counts. Potatoes, onions and carrots are cheap and store well, and are often best bought, but delicious early potatoes, spring onions and baby carrots ought to be eaten within hours of picking. In the shops, their flavour and texture quickly deteriorate.

What crops to grow?

First of all, consider your needs. Do you really want to grow crops that are readily available, cheap and tasty, to buy? It's probably better to concentrate on your favourite exotic varieties, or those that are expensive to buy – pumpkins or asparagus – or the ones that taste so much better eaten fresh, like tomatoes. Once you have made a list of what you like, decide how much you need. Remember that growing too little is better than growing too much and then having to discard produce that you have spent time and money nurturing.

Next, consider the soil. If you haven't created raised beds filled with decent soil and have cold, clay ground, then early crops will be tricky to grow because the soil is slow to warm up. However, later crops should be abundant, and will need relatively little watering. Light soil, on the other hand, is good for producing early crops but can be dry and unproductive later. So if you have clay soil, consider raising early crops in containers; if you have light soil, growing late-maturing crops in shallow trenches so that you can give them a good watering.

Then think about how much time and effort your plants will need. Upright tomatoes, for example, need staking, training and protecting from blight, and they crop outdoors for only a few weeks in late summer, while runner beans crop abundantly over a long period. On the other hand, asparagus almost looks after itself, and once you have established a bed it needs only routine annual maintenance in exchange for up to ten years of abundant produce. If you prefer to avoid periods of intense work, choose crops that need sowing, planting, thinning and weeding over a long period so the work is spread out Finally, consider the timing of the harvest. Make sure you plan crops that will be ready for picking all through the year.

Buying seeds and plug plants

Check the catalogues and websites of suppliers of vegetable seeds and plug plants. Since seed can be stored in cool, dark, dry conditions, it is worth buying in as wide a selection as you have room for, saving surplus seed for future years. Seed packets usually have some kind of expiry date and, though it is true that old seeds are less likely to germinate than new ones, they are likely to be viable for several years. To help you choose vegetables, the RHS regularly tests different kinds and publishes lists of recommended varieties on its website (www.rhs.org.uk/plants), giving its Award of Garden Merit (AGM) to the very best. AGM plants do not require highly specialist growing conditions or care.

A LARGE PLOT allows for plenty of scope, but still needs careful planning for year-round cropping.

Early spring

Clean start Double check that old crops and weeds have been removed.

Weeds Hoe young weeds the moment they appear. It is worth preparing the seedbed just to encourage weed seeds to germinate so that you can kill them now. Once the surface weed seeds have germinated and been removed, few others will sprout and you will have a clean bed.

Raking As soon as the soil is dry enough, rake it level and create a fine tilth.

Feeding Most vegetable gardens need feeding. Once the winter rains have stopped, spread general-purpose fertilizer in the recommended proportions.

Germination rates The soil is still often rather cold yet for good results. If in doubt, wait until weeds begin to emerge; when they germinate, so will your seed. It is better to wait a week or two than to sow in poor conditions.

Soil covering To keep the soil weed-free and moist, ready for sowing, cover it with black polythene.

Containers Fill containers with compost, ready for sowing vegetables.

Sowing in the ground

Broad beans, calabrese, early carrots, lettuces, onions, parsley, parsnips, peas, radishes, rocket, salsify, scorzonera, spinach, spring onions, turnips and herbs such as dill and chervil, can all be sown where they are to grow. If frost and winds are a problem, cover the sown area with horticultural fleece or cloches.

EARLY SPRING is the time to start sowing the first seeds in the ground.

Carrots and cabbages All carrot and cabbage-related crops benefit from a fleece covering to exclude soil pests, cabbage root fly and carrot fly, which are on the wing in mid-spring.

Successional sowing Once the first sowings are a few centimetres tall it is time, in many cases, to make further sowings to get a continuous supply of crops. Peas crop for about two weeks in summer; to cover the whole period you can sow up to four times in spring for a regular supply. Since salad crops become unappetising very quickly, sow seed little and often.

Watering With the soil still moist from winter, you seldom need to water in spring, but cold dry winds can parch seedbeds, so light watering is helpful.

Thinning As soon as seedlings can be handled, start thinning them out where they are too thick and, where appropriate, transplant to fill gaps.

Greenhouse sowing Ideally in a greenhouse, or indoors, sow aubergines, beetroot, celeriac, celery, peppers (including chillies), tomatoes and tender herbs (such as basil).

Transplanting Raise Brussels sprouts, leeks, summer cabbages and cauliflowers in pots, cell trays indoors or an outdoor seedbed for transplanting seedlings to their final position later in spring.

Crowns, tubers and sets Plant asparagus crowns, tubers of early potatoes and Jerusalem artichokes, and onion sets and shallots.

Ordering If you have decided not to raise your own plants from seed, order plug plants from mail-order suppliers as early as possible.

Poor results Failures will occur. If this happens, sow again with fresh seed. This is why you should always hold some seed in reserve.

Pests Apply slug controls to protect seedlings. The sudden disappearance of pea and bean seed indicates the presence of mice, so they will need to be trapped. Nets will help exclude birds from seedbeds, where they can be very destructive.

HOE AS YOU GO. Remove the heads of weeds as they emerge to give your young plants the best advantage.

Late spring

Second batch By late spring the main sowing season for hardy vegetables is over, except where planting successive sowings for a continuous supply is needed. However, there are still important crops to come. Beetroot, calabrese, carrots, lettuces, onions, parsley, parsnips, late peas, radishes, rocket, swedes, spinach, spring onions, turnips and herbs (such as parsley, dill and chervil) can be sown in the ground where they are to grow.

Successional sowings Remember that by the time these crops mature in later summer you will want less of them because tender crops, including French beans and tomatoes, will then be ready. And in the heat of midsummer the likes of lettuce, spinach and radish won't stay in good condition for more than a few days but will quickly deteriorate.

Transplants Raise transplants, including cabbages and cauliflowers for autumn, spring and winter, and purple sprouting broccoli, in pots, cell trays under glass or a seedbed outdoors.

Tender, frost-sensitive crops Sow courgettes, cucumbers, French beans, marrows, melons, pumpkins, squash and sweetcorn under glass. All have large seed which produces fast-growing plants, so sow only when the date of the last frost is no more than six weeks away, or you will have plants waiting to be planted out while frosts still threaten.

Hardening off Many of the transplants sown earlier in spring will be ready to go outdoors after hardening off. Brussels sprouts, salads, summer calabrese, cauliflowers and cabbages in particular appreciate early planting out, even if a temporary fleece covering is required in cold snaps.

Greenhouse plants Tender crops, such as aubergines, peppers and tomatoes, can be planted in greenhouse borders or growbags. Those for growing outside need a few more weeks under glass before being moved out.

Buying In plants If you have not raised your own plants, garden centres are usually well stocked with small pots of tender and other crops. The best ones sell quickly, and those that don't soon deteriorate

under garden centre conditions, so buy as soon as possible even if you have to keep them under fleece or on a sunny windowsill until you are ready to plant.

Catching up There is still time to sow and plant any crops that should have been raised earlier in spring. They invariably catch up. In fact, with badly drained gardens in cold exposed sites it is worth waiting until late spring; early sowing is too risky.

Pest protection By now, crops should be pushing up well. Since carrots, parsnips and cabbage-related crops are still vulnerable to pests, keep them covered with fleece or insect-proof nets for as long as possible.

Support Peas need to be provided with sticks or mesh to climb up, and broad beans often need support from stakes and string.

Potatoes Earth up potatoes as shoots emerge to prevent the tubers from turning green.

Weeding Weed growth is at its peak. Hoeing on dry days reduces hand weeding to a minimum.

Thinning Crops can be growing very fast, so thinning is a priority to avoid spoiling all the hard work you've already invested.

Smart and beautiful Vegetable plots should look good, so keep weeding and tidying edges and paths, and removing debris. Tidiness helps prevent accidents in the garden (leaving less around for you to lose or trip over), and deprives slugs and other pests of shelter.

Early summer

First crop The first baby carrots, beetroot, broad beans, salads and peas, and so on are ready in early summer. Since their freshness declines with age, harvest immediately. This also frees the space for later crops.

Act early Long days, moist soil, warm temperatures and a high sun give excellent growth. By late summer conditions are much less favourable, so it makes sense to get everything planted and in full growth well before midsummer.

Keep planting As space becomes available, lightly cultivate the ground, add fertilizer, and sow or plant.

Outdoor sowing Courgettes, cucumbers, French beans, marrows, melons, pumpkins, runner beans, squashes and sweetcorn can be sown outdoors in sheltered, mild districts, where they are to grow. Being sown in the ground, they develop superior roots systems which help them grow fast; they won't require as much watering as transplants. All remaining hardy plants, including cabbages, cauliflowers, celery, celeriac, broccoli and leeks, should be planted out as soon as possible.

Tender plants raised under glass They can also be planted out after hardening off. A fleece covering is a big help in boosting growth in cool districts. Aubergines, melons and peppers seldom thrive without extra protection outdoors.

Avoiding bolting By the end of early summer, crops that bolt if they encounter cold nights and/or short days can be sown. These include chicory, endive, Florence fennel and Oriental greens like Chinese cabbage.

Extra sowing In warm districts, it is worth sowing crops like French beans, runner beans, and courgettes in cell trays to plant out as soil becomes free in late summer.

Earthing up Potatoes can be given their final earthing up.

Staking Canes and stakes should be inserted in good time to support taller crops such as runner beans and tomatoes.

TIE IN tall plants like vine tomatoes and climbing beans.

Weeding Weed growth should slow down in summer, but survivors of a spring weeding session will need pulling out before they can set flower and scatter their seed.

Feeding Giving crops more fertilizer is often worthwhile. Greedy cabbage family plants, beetroot, celery, celeriac and leeks, however, benefit from supplementary feeding. Container-grown vegetables benefit from a regular liquid feed.

Pest protection Erect netting to protect peas and cabbage family crops against hungry pigeons. Also use discs to fend off cabbage root fly and take precautions against carrot fly. Insect pests, including blackfly, caterpillars, greenfly and leaf mining insects, begin to cause damage in summer. Red spider mite thrives in hot, dry conditions causing leaf loss on French beans, runner beans and crops under glass. If damage threatens to become significant, act promptly.

Diseases From midsummer, blight is a constant menace, requiring frequent protective spraying for potatoes and tomatoes. In dry seasons, powdery mildew can be damaging to courgettes, cucumbers, peas, pumpkins and swedes. Careful watering to keep the soil moist can limit damage.

Late summer

Frequent picking The more you pick courgettes, beans and tomatoes, the more will be produced.

Herbs Keep removing the flowers on herbs to gain extra leaves.

Garlic, onions and shallots The leaves will turn yellow and topple, and the produce can be gathered, dried and stored.

Harvest quickly Clear spent crops promptly to eliminate pests and diseases, and expose weeds.

Beans and tomatoes Train growth to supports. Nip out side shoots and tops of upright tomatoes (not the bush types), and pinch out the tops of climbing beans as they reach the top of their support.

Sprouts and broccoli Tall winter crops like Brussels sprouts and purple sprouting broccoli can be earthed up or staked to secure them against winter gales.

Extra crops As soil becomes free, sow quick-growing crops of beetroot, French beans, kohl rabi, radishes, winter salad leaves and turnips. Plant out seedlings raised in early summer. Also plant new potatoes for autumn, although blight can be damaging in a wet, warm autumn. Finally, sow next spring's cabbages, leaf beet and spring onions.

Pest and diseases Attacks often decrease in hot, dry weather, but caterpillars can be very damaging to cabbage family crops if they are allowed to develop. Potato blight remains a risk in wet periods. Affected potato crops should have their foliage removed and disposed of; the potatoes should be lifted two weeks later. Don't ignore carrot fly – it's still a potential problem and an infestation can ruin the roots.

Potatoes As soon as they are ready, store in a dark, cool place to avoid slug damage.

Green manures If you have spare time and space and the soil is sufficiently moist, sow fodder radish, fenugreek, and mustard, for example, to improve soil fertility and the workability of stiff ground.

PINCH OUT sideshoots and tops of vine tomatoes to concentrate growth on the fruit.

ENJOY THE HARVEST. Crops are best harvested when they are young and sweet; this will also promote further cropping.

Autumn

Harvesting Cut down the dying tops of potatoes before storing the crop. Remove the dying tops of pumpkins and squashes, and cure the fruit in a warm, sunny place for a week or two before storing in a dry, frost-free place. Autumn cabbages, calabrese, cauliflower, celery, endive and chicory are ready for harvesting. Summer crops like beans and tomatoes are finished and should be consigned to the compost bin. Remove, clean and store their cane supports.

Clearing up Remove spent stems and debris to avoid harbouring pests and diseases, and to expose slugs and other pests to the birds and weather.

Root vegetables Most are best left in the ground and gathered as you need them, but in case a cold spell prevents harvesting or even damages them, a proportion can be lifted and stored in a frost-free shed. Celeriac and turnips are especially frost-sensitive. Carrots left in the ground benefit from being insulated under straw or cardboard, with a plastic sheet to shed rain.

Spring cabbages Transplant to their final positions. Plant over-wintered onion sets, and sow over-wintered lettuces and spinach. Later, hardy pea and broad bean cultivars can be sown in the ground in sheltered districts with well-drained soil. Cloches provide winter protection, if required. And just before winter sets in, plant garlic and shallots.

Green manures There is still time to sow green manures, including Italian ryegrass, grazing rye and vetches, which establish in autumn, survive winter and are ready for digging in early next spring.

BOTTOM: TIDY AWAY old plants once they finish cropping and add them to the compost heap.

INSET: WORMERIES are good for small gardens that produce just small amounts of waste.

Winter

IMPROVE YOUR SOIL by adding plenty of well-rotted organic matter such as your own garden compost.

Pre-spring checks Dig over vacant ground, spread organic manures, incorporate green manures, check the pH and add lime if required, and make sure the soil is in the best condition for an early start next spring. Keep weeding.

Harvesting Gather winter vegetables and use those in store, discarding anything rotten.

Compost Empty compost bins, mix the contents and refill them.

Planning and ordering Draw up plans for next year's vegetable garden, and order seed packets. Check you'll have sufficient canes, stakes, netting, fertilizer and pesticides. Bear in mind that mail-order suppliers and gardening clubs and societies can offer significant savings over retail outlets.

Storing seed When seed arrives, store in cool, dark, dry conditions. Lay out potato tubers to sprout or 'chit'.

Buying plants It is sometimes more convenient to buy plants in spring than to take the trouble of raising your own early transplants.

Waiting for spring By late winter there is an almost irresistible temptation to start sowing and planting. You can begin sowing early crops under glass, however, either on a windowsill or in a glasshouse. Unless your garden is unusually well-drained and in a sheltered, mild district, wait for the warm weather of spring before planting anything.

Raising under glass Broad beans, Brussels sprouts, early summer cabbage, calabrese, cauliflowers, leeks, onions, peas, radishes, shallots, spinach and turnips can be raised under cover. Windowsills are rather dark and seedlings suffer if grown on them for prolonged periods. Greenhouses offer better conditions, but some heating is needed to produce healthy, well-grown plants.

Rhubarb and Jerusalem artichokes Plant out.

Growing your own

- Garlic, leeks, onions and shallots
- Cabbage family
- Beans and peas
- Perennial vegetables
- Root and stem vegetables
- Salads
- Spinach and chard
- Squashes, marrows, pumpkins and sweetcorn
- Tender vegetables

Garlic, leeks, onions and shallots

With their wonderful spherical shape and layers of flesh sheathed in a thin golden skin, onions are a masterpiece of natural design. Gentle cooking brings out the aromatic taste of sweet shallots – ideal for popping into vegetable stews. Garlic, whose juicy fresh bulbs are the most flavoursome of all, is traditionally planted on the shortest day, the winter solstice, and harvested on the longest, the summer solstice. A robust crop, it demands little effort to grow and suffers from few problems. Leeks, a wonderfully tasty addition to many dishes, can be harvested all through winter and early spring.

Garlic

It is indicative of the sea change in our cooking that over the last 20 years garlic has become one of the must-grow crops in the British vegetable plot. There are gardeners here who have grown it for much longer, but it is only now commonplace. Few crops are as easy and satisfying to grow. Each separate clove planted in the ground will yield, just a few months later, a great clump of 20 more.

Despite its associations with Mediterranean cuisine and Indian and Chinese cooking, garlic is perfectly suited to cultivation in the cooler climes of the British Isles. While our own wild garlic thrives in damp, shady woodland, cultivated culinary garlic must have sun. The more it gets, the faster it develops and the chunkier the bulbs grow.

The process of planting garlic could not be simpler. Lower Individual cloves into holes deep enough to hide their tips under an inch of soil, and firm in gently. This encourages roots to grow rapidly and, at this stage of any bulb's existence, that is the most important task; only when a good root system has developed can nutrients and water be transported into the bulb. You can plant in early autumn for harvesting from early summer onwards, or plant a later crop, say in late winter or early spring, to reach maturity later in summer. When the leaves begin to shrivel, gently pull the bulb from the soil and leave it on the surface if the weather is hot, or raised on chicken wire if the weather is wet. If rain is forecast, cover it. When the outside skin is really papery and thoroughly dry you can plait the bunches or hang them in a dry, airy place.

Green garlic is now fashionable and, far from being some mysterious and difficult-to-grow crop, it is simply garlic that has been lifted while it is still growing, with its leaves still green. Just lift a whole bulb, separate a few cloves and, when you are ready to use it, squeeze it out of its papery covering, new and pristine. It has a much milder flavour than older, stored garlic, and a creamier texture. It can be baked whole with other vegetables or baked, crushed and added to toppings based on chickpeas or puréed beans.

Garlic's health-giving and healing properties have been recognized for millennia, and there are references to its medicinal properties in texts from Roman, Egyptian and other ancient civilizations. But whether you are growing it for health or for the kitchen, from summer until the end of the autumn after it has been lifted it retains its fresh, creamy quality. It will last beyond that, especially if you use 'long dormancy' varieties, but the flavour begins to change, becoming stronger and harder.

GARLIC BULBS can spring up unexpectedly if left in the ground from a previous crop. Bees love them.

Garlic *Allium sativum*

Garlic is one of the oldest and most valued of plants. Pliny the Elder listed over 60 ailments curable by garlic – and so potent are its properties that the ancients believed it had supernatural powers. It is extremely easy to grow, and produces so many fat, juicy bulbs that it will transform your cooking and you won't ever want to go back to shop-bought garlic.

	J	F	M	A	M	J	J	A	S	O	N	D
Plant	■	■								■	■	■
Harvest						■	■	■				

The best sites and soils

Because warmth is needed to ripen the bulbs, garlic must be grown in a sunny site, in rich soil that is moisture-retentive but with good drainage. Avoid planting on freshly manured ground which could cause rotting.

Planting cloves

While garlic can be planted any time from mid-autumn to late winter, the best yields are obtained if planting is completed before Christmas. On heavy ground that could become waterlogged, make a raised ridge of soil to plant on, or start off cloves in modular trays in a greenhouse or cold frame for transplanting outside in late winter. Just before planting, thoroughly rake the top few centimetres of soil and incorporate a general fertilizer. Gently split the bulb into individual cloves, and use a trowel or

PLANT EACH GARLIC CLOVE in the ground with its pointed tip uppermost and about 2.5cm below the surface.

dibber to plant each one with the pointed end uppermost, spaced 10cm (4in) apart with 23–30cm (9–12in) between rows. The tips of the cloves should be hidden just below the surface. Firm in gently.

Recommended varieties

Purple Wight
An early variety with purple-streaked bulbs that can be harvested from the end of June. It is best used fresh as it does not store well.

Spanish Roja
An old variety that is keenly sought for its strong, distinctive flavour. The medium-sized bulbs store well and the cloves are easy to peel.

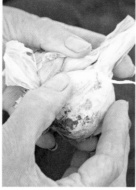

WHEN HARVESTING GARLIC, cut off the stems of the bulbs unless you plan to plait them together.

ONCE THE BULBS have dried out, you can gently split some of the individual cloves apart for planting your next crop.

Cultivating the crop

For the first month or so after planting, regularly check the crop for signs of bird or animal damage; any uprooted bulbs need to be pushed back before they dry out. As garlic is shallow rooting, it dislikes competition and the ground should be weeded regularly – taking care not to damage the bulbs. During spring and early summer, an occasional thorough watering during dry spells will improve the yield. Don't water once the bulbs are large and well formed, because this could encourage rotting.

At harvest time

The earliest varieties mature from late spring to early summer, while most mature around late summer. Plants are ready to harvest when the stems begin to yellow and bend over. Use a fork to loosen the bulbs from the soil, and then spread them out in the sun to dry, ideally on wire mesh or netting so that the air can circulate around them. Keep them dry.

Storing and cooking tips

To store bulbs, gently knock off the dry soil and place in a net bag or plait the stems to form a rope of bulbs. Although a garlic rope in the kitchen makes an attractive decoration, a cool, dry shed or garage is by far the best place for storage. When adding garlic to the likes of a stir-fry, don't let it burn in hot oil because it becomes bitter.

Pests and diseases

Disease is unlikely in good growing conditions, but mould or rust may occur during long, wet spells. Any badly affected bulbs should be thrown away or burnt immediately.

If the foliage yellows and wilts, look for the fluffy, white growths of onion white rot on the bulbs. Throw out any infected ones, and it would be a good idea to avoid growing garlic or onions in the same site again for eight years, to give this persistent disease time to die out.

GARLIC'S SPECIAL PROPERTIES

Garlic is a powerful antibacterial with over 30 active compounds. Allicin gives the characteristic smell. Before modern antibiotics, garlic was commonly used to treat wounds and it is still widely used to treat antibiotic-resistant infections.

Californian Late
This popular North American late variety produces fairly large bulbs that store well. The cloves have a rich, almost sweet taste.

Solent White AGM
Very attractive, late-maturing bulbs with a good yield. The bulbs will store well into the following spring.

Leeks *Allium porrum*

Grown for its stem-like rolled leaves, the leek is a versatile and useful vegetable that's easy to grow in the right soil conditions. But 'easy' doesn't mean low maintenance: leeks need transplanting and some earthing up. They may occupy the ground for a long time, but their big advantage is that they can be harvested over a long period – from autumn to late winter.

	J	F	M	A	M	J	J	A	S	O	N	D
Sow	■	■	■	■								
Plant				■	■	■						
Harvest	■	■	■	■				■	■	■	■	■

The best sites and soils

Leeks do best in a sunny site on any reasonable soil that doesn't become waterlogged in winter, although the ideal soil is heavy and moisture-retentive. On drier, free-draining ground it's important to add plenty of well-rotted organic matter to produce a good crop. Dig the planting site in autumn or winter and leave it rough in clods, then rake over before planting, and incorporate a general fertilizer.

Using seed and set

Leeks are a transplanted crop that can be sown in containers or in a seedbed before being moved to their final growing position.

They are easy to raise from seed, but if you miss the sowing time or run out of space, it's possible to buy ready-grown young plants during the spring and early summer.

To get an early crop to mature from late summer to autumn, sow in a seed tray from mid- to late winter in a heated greenhouse or on a windowsill. Prick out the seedlings into modular trays or space them 5cm

ABOVE: AFTER TRANSPLANTING, water the young leek plants thoroughly. Repeat during long, dry spells – but sparingly.

LEFT: HOE YOUR LEEK bed regularly to keep the weeds at bay.

(2in) apart, and continue growing them under cover before hardening them off in a cold frame for planting out in mid-spring.

Alternatively, sow in a seedbed outside from early to mid-spring for plants to mature in autumn, or in early to mid-summer for plants to stay in the ground, and harvest the following spring. Rake the soil to a fine tilth and sow thinly in drills 15cm (6in) apart and 1cm (½in) deep.

The time to transplant is when the young leeks are about pencil thick. Water thoroughly the day before transplanting and lift using a fork. Make wide, deep holes – 15cm (6in) deep and 5cm (2in) across – and drop a single seedling in each. Don't backfill with soil, but simply fill each hole with water to settle the soil around the roots.

Cultivating the crop

Planting leeks in deep holes will produce white shafts of a good length, but for even longer ones earth up by gradually piling soil around the stems during the growing season. Weed regularly, preferably using a hoe. During long, dry spells, water thoroughly but sparingly – a good soaking every 10 days will do.

At harvest time

Leeks are simple to harvest; just lift them as required when the stems are sufficiently thick, and trim the leaves and roots. 'Baby' leeks for salads can be pulled from early summer, although it's more usual to wait for the stems to thicken to ensure a harvest of good-sized plants from late summer for soups, casseroles and other dishes.

Storing and cooking tips

Wash thoroughly before use by slicing in half lengthways and holding upside-down under running water so any dirt washes out easily. Take care when cooking leeks in hot oil: like garlic, they can burn easily and become bitter. Cook them gently until they are soft and translucent.

Pests and diseases

Leek rust, seen as orange pustules, is a disease that may occur in damp weather. When harvesting leeks, make sure that you throw away or burn any affected leaves and, in future, choose a resistant variety for sowing. Look for varieties that have some resistance to disease.

Recommended varieties

Carlton AGM
A early-maturing variety that grows strongly and has good taste. The seeds germinate quickly and yields are high.

Apollo AGM
Expect high yields from December with this blue-green leek. It has good resistance to rust.

Toledo AGM
An excellent leek with much longer shafts than other varieties. The yields are high and late in the season.

Pancho AGM
A good early yield of rust-resistant leeks with long, solid shafts with good taste.

Onions

" How could we cook without onions? They are the mainstay of every global cuisine, and in the past they were treasured even more highly. The ancient Egyptians worshipped them, their spherical shape and layer after layer of skin symbolizing eternal life. Onions made from gold were used as effigies in burial ceremonies, and the onion was represented in wall paintings and bas relief in pyramids of both the Old and New Kingdoms. And, of course, onions were held in high esteem because of their antiseptic properties, and both onions and garlic are still used as herbal medicines.

Onions and radishes were the two main foods cultivated and consumed by the workers who built the pyramids. In ancient Greece, athletes ate onions and Roman gladiators rubbed them into their bodies to harden their muscles. In England, in the Middle Ages, onions, cabbages and beans were the three main staples. They are rich in vitamins and minerals, can be stored and kept from harvest to harvest, and are reliable and easy-going to grow.

Harvesting onions is one of my favourite jobs. There is a wonderful moment when you realize that all those luscious green stems have toppled over, as if they've given their all. You can bend the tops over yourself, but there is something magical about

HARVESTING ONIONS is a special experience – as they dry in the sun, the crisp scales flake away.

seeing this spontaneous collapse. In hot sunny weather, the leaves eventually wither and become crisp. Pulling the fat bulbs from the soil and laying them with their bases facing the sun to dry out is magical. It completes the cycle.

Provided they have sun, onions will produce a crop practically anywhere. There are two ways to plant them: sets, the small, specially prepared onions, produce leaves that die back during summer after the bulb has swelled; seeds can be sown into the ground, or into trays or pots for transplanting into the ground when they are big enough.

Sets are available in early spring, and in early autumn you can find sets of winter onions which will grow through the coldest months to give a new crop in early summer. Maincrop sets can be planted out as soon as the soil is in reasonable condition.

There is no need to plant or sow them successionally because they keep so well. Plant your sets as early as possible, and keep them growing well with an occasional feed.

I love cooking with onions. Just handling the solid round bulbs is a sensual experience. How can such a thin skin protect all that succulence? Red onions, milder in flavour, are particularly prized raw in salads or as a garnish. Finely sliced with tomatoes, they make a simple, classic dish. "

Onions and shallots

Allium cepa and *Allium cepa* (Aggregatum Group)

In the kitchen, onions and shallots must be the most frequently used vegetable. They are used as seasoning in dishes ranging from sauces to soups to salads. They are grown in much the same way, although shallots grow to form clusters of small bulbs. Shallots are one of the easiest crops. They mature early, freeing up the ground for follow-on crops.

	J	F	M	A	M	J	J	A	S	O	N	D
Plant sets			•						•	•		•
Harvest					•	•	•	•	•	•		

The best sites and soils

Grow in a sunny, sheltered site in soil that is moisture-retentive but has good drainage. While a soil rich in organic matter produces good crops and is particularly important for seed-raised onions, avoid planting on freshly manured ground because this is said to lead to rotting. Although you should avoid growing onions on the same site every year (pests and diseases can build up in the soil), you can try growing them on the same plot until disease strikes and then move them on.

Using seed and sets

The easiest and quickest way to raise onions and shallots is by planting sets, or baby onions. Being partly developed already, they grow rapidly and are particularly useful when the growing season is short. Sets are usually planted from early to mid-spring to crop from mid- to late summer. Hardy Japanese varieties can also be planted in autumn for an early summer crop the following year – as long as your soil isn't prone to waterlogging. Just before planting, thoroughly rake the top few centimetres of soil and incorporate a general fertilizer. Mark out rows 25–30cm (10–12in) apart, and push the sets into the soil with 7.5–10cm (3–4in) between each one, the pointed end uppermost and the tip just visible. Shallots need earlier planting and wider spacing. Plant them just before spring, spacing the bulbs 15cm (6in) apart with 25–30cm (10–12in) between rows.

Onions and shallots can also be grown from seed sown in spring, as soon as the soil is workable, to give a late summer crop, or in late summer for an early summer crop the following year. Sow thinly in rows 30cm (12in) apart, and thin to the above spacings.

THE BULBS begin to swell during early summer. It is essential to keep them well watered and free from weeds at this stage in the plants' development.

Cultivating the crop

Birds or frost can lift the bulbs out of the soil. Cover with fleece if this is a problem. Onions and shallots are shallow rooting, and should be weeded regularly to avoid competition for water and food. The ideal tool is a short-handled onion hoe which gives good control, but it's best to hand-weed closely around the bulbs to avoid any damage. Cultivation of shallots is exactly the same as for onions. Plant at the end of winter or beginning of spring.

The bulbs grow mostly during the coolest part of the year, sending their roots down into the soil to pull up water and nutrients. During summer, the roots contract and gradually all the goodness from the top foliage is channelled into the bulbs making them swell, and pushing them out from the centre helping them to ripen.

FRESHLY HARVESTED SHALLOTS, separated into their individual bulbs and laid out in the sun to dry. The roots and shoots will shrivel up and can be trimmed off before storing.

Recommended varieties (onions)

Setton AGM
One of the best varieties with excellent yields of dark-skinned bulbs that store well.

Sturon AGM
A popular and reliable variety well known for its flavour and medium-sized bulbs that store well over winter.

Centurion AGM
A top-class, strong-growing variety that gives a heavy, early maturing crop. The straw-coloured bulbs are slightly flattened and store well.

Hercules AGM
As the name suggests, these large bulbs with dark golden skins are exceptional. Expect good yields. Stores well.

Forum
A very early-maturing variety with fat bulbs that are ready to harvest not long after midsummer. They do not store beyond autumn.

Hyred
A late-maturing red onion with attractive crimson bulbs. They store well over winter.

LIFTING ONIONS AND SHALLOTS

1 ONIONS AND SHALLOTS can be lifted as soon as you need them, although they store better if allowed to die back first.

2 PUSH A GARDEN FORK under the plants and lever the soil up as you pull the bulb out of the ground by its neck.

3 BULBS CAN BE LEFT to dry out in the sun or taken directly to the kitchen for immediate use.

At harvest time

Both onions and shallots are ready to harvest when the leaves begin to yellow; around mid- to late July for shallots, and early to late summer for onions, depending on the sowing or planting time. You can even take one or two shallot bulbs out while they are in growth to use fresh, without disturbing the rest. For the general harvest, use a fork to loosen the

THE IDEAL WAY to dry bulbs is to lay them out in the sun, either on wire mesh or trays raised above the ground, which reduces the chances of them rotting.

bulbs from the soil, and then spread the bulbs out in the sun to dry, ideally on wire mesh above the ground so that air can circulate around them. Separate shallots into individual bulbs first.

Storing and cooking tips

Once the bulbs are thoroughly dry, gently knock off any loose soil and leaves, and then store them in a net bag and keep in a cool, dry shed or garage. At this stage they are packed with vitamins and minerals.The skins are brown and papery, and the remnants of stems and leaves also make a convenient tool for bunching or plaiting them together, and hanging them ready for use.

In the kitchen shallots can be used raw, in salads or as a garnish, thinly sliced with a very sharp knife. They should always be cut in this way, since if shallots are chopped roughly they can get bruised at the edges and lose some of their flavour. Shallots are delicious baked whole, glazed with balsamic vinegar and oil or butter with a pinch of sugar, and can be added to many sauces.

The taste of shallots is unique – intense, sweet and aromatic, making them especially popular for cooking in vegetable stews, but they are never acrid in the way that onions and stored garlic can be.

Pests and diseases

Disease should be minimal given good growing conditions, but mildew may occur during long, wet spells. Picking off affected leaves can sometimes save the crop but they won't keep as long as uninfected bulbs. If the foliage turns yellow and wilts, look for the symptoms of onion white rot on the bulbs (fluffy, white growths). Destroy any infected ones, and avoid growing onions and garlic on the same site for eight years after that to make sure that the disease has had time to die out. Rotating the crop on to a different site each year also avoids the build-up of eelworms.

BULBS SHOWING SIGNS of damage or disease must not be stored. Either put them aside for immediate use or discard or destroy them if the damage is bad.

Recommended varieties (shallots)

Longor AGM
Like the name suggests, these are long bulbs. They store well and have a good flavour and yield. Suitable for showing.

Jermor AGM
The large crops of copper-skinned bulbs are highly rated for their flavour. Popular with exhibitors.

Hative de Niort
A very attractive variety with pear-shaped bulbs that are quite popular with exhibitors.

Santé AGM
A good variety for the kitchen with a mild flavour. Produces high yields of uniform reddish-brown bulbs suitable for exhibiting. Plant out after mid-spring (more likely to bolt if planted too early).

Delvad AGM
A top-quality shallot with good yields of round, flavoursome bulbs.

Pikant AGM
A well-known, early maturing shallot with strong flavour and high yields. The bulbs store well.

Cabbage family

Members of the cabbage family are commonly known to vegetable growers as brassicas. They are among the most useful of all vegetable crops, providing a fresh, nutritious harvest all year round, and they're particularly welcome from winter to early spring when there is little else available in the garden. The group includes those vegetables often collectively known as 'greens', such as cabbages and kale, Brussels sprouts, broccoli and cauliflower. All share similar growing requirements, and for the sake of practicality they're often found growing side-by-side in the vegetable garden.

PUDDLING IN is traditional when planting brassicas – place the plant in the hole and fill with water several times before adding soil and firming well.

KEEP BRASSICAS FREE of competing weeds by regular hoeing and hand weeding. Remove any root collars that have been put in place, and take care not to damage the vulnerable stems.

Different types of brassica

Cabbage exists in many guises, grouped according to its season. Savoy, white and red cabbages are usually listed separately by catalogues, although they are grown as winter cabbages. Broccoli and cauliflower are grown for their flowering heads.

The Italian word broccoli means 'little sprouts'. The familiar vegetable with chunky, cauliflower-like heads of tiny flowers is more accurately known as calabrese, and it can be harvested from midsummer into autumn.

The other broccoli is the sprouting type, which is available from mid-winter to mid-spring. This produces either purple or white flowerheads, the former having a more intense, peppery flavour. Many gardeners depend on this useful, late-winter staple to follow Brussels sprouts when there's little else around.

Cauliflowers have a reputation for being tricky to grow, but time spent on soil preparation and plenty of watering throughout the growing season will reap rewards. True cauliflowers bear the characteristic creamy white heads commonly known as curds. There are also hybrids that bear purple, lime-green and even orange heads.

The best sites and soils

Brassicas love a sunny spot and thrive on firm soil improved with generous quantities of organic matter such as well-rotted manure or garden compost.

Whenever possible, prepare the soil in autumn, giving it time to consolidate over winter. Before transplanting brassicas onto the site, check that the soil is well firmed by shuffling along its entire surface on your heels, then rake it flat. Avoid digging at this stage. Inadequate soil anchorage is often the reason for poor development of the crop. As the plant develops, support any unstable stems with a 5 x 2.5cm (2 x 1in) wooden stake.

Sowing and planting

Although many seed catalogues and garden centres offer young plants ready for planting in their final positions, brassicas are easily raised from seed. If you don't have room for a seedbed, or just want a few plants to fill gaps in the border, or find that slugs and snails are a problem, sow the seed in modules.

Choose a modular tray with small, individual sections (those designed for raising 'plug' plants are ideal), and fill with multipurpose compost. Lightly firm the surface using the bottom of another tray, then sow two or three seeds per section, lightly covering with sieved soil. Water gently using a rose spray, then stand in a bright, sheltered, outdoor position under fleece to exclude cabbage root fly. Thin the seedlings to one plant per cell by nipping out the others with your fingertips. They can be transplanted into larger pots before being planted out.

Traditionally, brassica plants are raised in seedbeds for later transplanting to their final positions. This is because sowing each crop at its final spacing would take up a great deal of room early in the growing season when the ground could be used for fast-maturing crops such as lettuce. However, planting brassicas after midsummer greatly reduces yields of autumn crops and Brussels sprouts.

Pests and diseases

A number of pests and diseases can affect brassicas, and they're often easier to prevent than cure. Crop rotation, good soil preparation and care of the plants will lessen the likelihood of many problems.

Crop rotation reduces the build-up of soil-borne diseases and disorders; brassicas shouldn't be grown in the same position within two years. In the rotation cycle, brassicas normally follow beans and onions, which allows plenty of time for autumn preparation of the brassica bed. The brassicas also benefit from the extra nitrogen peas and beans add to the soil.

Avoid acid soil, which promotes the fungal disease clubroot. Liming the soil, providing good drainage, for instance, by using raised beds, and using plants raised in 15cm (6in) pots can allow fairly good crops to be grown even if clubroot is present.

The best defence against the three main brassica pests – caterpillars, the cabbage root fly and pigeons, is enclosing the plants in a cage covered by insect-proof netting. This is best put in place on planting, before insect pests begin to lay their eggs, or pigeons can peck at, or uproot, the seedlings.

To prevent cabbage root fly, place a 7.5cm (3in) disc or collar of roofing felt or carpet underlay around the base of the stem when planting out to prevent it laying its eggs. Growing garlic or chives nearby is said to throw them off the scent. Discourage slugs and snails with a biological control such as Nemaslug, or use other non-biological controls, such beer traps or a barrier of crushed eggshells.

Brassicas need good amounts of space between the individual plants to allow air to circulate around them, which helps to prevent diseases from taking hold. For the same reason, it is also important to remove weeds and any old, withered foliage as they appear.

PROTECTIVE COVERINGS of fine or medium netting are fairly vital when growing brassicas, as they keep many of the common pests at bay – such as cabbage white butterfly caterpillars and pigeons.

BIRD-PROOF NETTING should be put in place if pigeons are known to be a problem. Watering can be done in the usual way, but weeding is made more difficult as the nets will need to be removed.

Broccoli and cauliflowers

" Broccoli, calabrese and cauliflowers are valued for their heads of immature flowers, tightly gathered into curds, which are harvested before they start opening into individual buds. Between them they offer a harvest that can last for months although, to my mind, broccoli is by far the most useful and enduring crop.

Broccoli makes a handsome vegetable with tall, sturdy stems standing erect through rain, hail and snow. A cold-season vegetable, it does well in our climate. Both white and purple sprouting broccoli stand for months right through the hardest days of winter, offering a crop of tight, crunchy heads at the end of winter into the early days of spring. Each sprig is like a magical miniature tree with its own trunk and head of leaves.

Cauliflowers are completely different. They can be damaged by hard frost and are more difficult to grow than broccoli, having more exacting requirements. If you don't get it right, they end up on the compost heap. But if they grow well, there is nothing more rewarding than folding back the

PLANTED IN THE SPRING or early summer, broccoli may stand in the ground well into the following year, so make sure it is well planted.

fresh green leaves to reveal tight, white curds, and cutting the stem to carry the cauliflower triumphantly back to the kitchen.

You can grow two crops of cauliflowers: one sown from mid-spring for the summer and autumn harvest, and one sown in midsummer for spring. Seed can be sown directly in the ground or into seed trays or modules. The point to stress is that crop rotation probably benefits brassicas more than any other crop. If you can grow them where legumes, such as peas and beans, were growing last year, the brassicas will benefit considerably.

When planting any brassica, do make sure that the ground is firm. Although walking on the soil destroys its structure, brassicas need firm planting, so don't be afraid to use your feet when planting to firm them in around the base of the stems. If brassicas work themselves loose, especially cauliflowers, calabrese and broccoli, they will develop poor root systems and leaf structure so that they flower prematurely and produce small, poor-quality heads. Check they're well fixed in the ground. "

Broccoli

Brassica oleracea (Italica Group)

The large green heads of calabrese or broccoli are familiar summer vegetables in the kitchen, although the more ornamental white, lime-green and purple varieties are much less common. Sprouting broccolis produce many smaller flowerheads from late winter to spring; they are a valuable early crop and when fresh can be boiled and eaten with butter like asparagus.

	J	F	M	A	M	J	J	A	S	O	N	D
Sow				▪	▪	▪	▪					
Plant						▪	▪	▪				
Harvest	▪	▪	▪	▪				▪	▪	▪	▪	▪

The best sites and soils

Broccoli likes full sun and a rich soil improved with generous quantities of organic matter. Check the soil is firm and has a pH of 6.5–7.5 (see page 21).

Sowing and planting

Young sprouting broccoli and calabrese plants are available in late spring from garden centres and seed catalogues, but are easily raised from seed. Sow sprouting broccoli in seedbeds or modules (see page 70) from mid-spring (early varieties) to midsummer (late varieties), ready for transplanting to the garden after a few months. Calabrese are best sown directly where they are to grow. Thoroughly prepare the seedbeds by forking over the soil and raking the surface to produce a fine, crumbly texture.

BROCCOLI HEADS are ready to cut when the buds are well developed but before the flowers actually open. Regular picking encourages more cropping.

Stretch a length of string as a guide, and draw out a straight 1cm (½in) deep drill by dragging a measuring rod, hoe or broom handle along the line. If the bottom of the drill is dry, lightly water first. Sprinkle the seed thinly along its length, and cover with soil, which should be gently firmed by lightly patting down. The seedlings should appear within 7–12 days.

Thin out seedbed-raised plants so that they are 7.5cm (3in) apart. Weed the seedbed regularly, either by hand or by carefully hoeing between the lines. Slugs and snails will quickly devour seedlings, so pay particular attention to their control. The seedlings can be moved to their final position when they are roughly 10–15cm (4–6in) high. Water the seedbed shortly before transplanting. Plants sown in the ground should be thinned to their final spacing. Ensure that the prepared planting site is well firmed by shuffling up and down all over it on your heels. Rake flat and repeat until no dips or hollows remain.

Leave 30cm (12in) between calabrese plants, and 45cm (18in) between purple and white sprouting plants and rows. The wide spacing will ensure good air circulation around the plants and help prevent diseases. Dig a hole big enough to accommodate the roots and deep enough for the lowest leaves to be near the soil surface. Plant seedlings 2.5cm (1in) deeper than in the seedbed to give them good anchorage, and water in. Net the crop against insects and pigeons.

Cultivating the crop

As the plants develop, make sure they never go short of water, which will prevent the formation of good flowering heads and could result in fungal diseases. Reduce competition for moisture and nutrients by carefully hoeing off the tops of weeds around the plants the moment they appear.

At harvest time

All types of broccoli should be picked when the flower shoots are well developed, but before the flowers actually open. Picking regularly and early will encourage side-shoot formation for further harvests. Cut the florets from the plant using a sharp knife, cutting the central spear first.

Green broccoli is ready to harvest from midsummer to mid-autumn, depending on the variety. Individual spears or the entire head of sprouting varieties can be harvested from late autumn. Harvest the flower shoots of the purple and white sprouting kinds from mid-winter to spring. Regular picking can extend the cropping time for up to eight weeks.

Storing and cooking tips

Broccoli is virtually fat-free and packed with vitamins C and E, fibre and iron – provided the florets are not overcooked. Florets will stay fresh in the refrigerator for about three days and they also freeze well. Stir-fry or lightly steam for maximum nutrients and flavour.

Pests and diseases

Regularly check plants for signs of caterpillars and pick any off or spray with derris dust. Alternatively, prevent butterflies from laying eggs by covering the crop with fine-grade netting on planting. Remove any yellowing or fallen leaves, and dispose of them to prevent the spread of fungal diseases.

Recommended varieties

Arcadia AGM
A plentiful crop of small dark green heads for cutting from late summer.

Belstar AGM
A medium- to late-season variety with many attractive, medium, blue-green heads. Good for organic use.

Fiesta AGM
Large, domed heads of consistent quality on plants that are tolerant of summer heat. Ready from early autumn.

Red Arrow AGM
A sprouting broccoli with heavy crops of claret-purple florets on tall stems over a long late-winter season.

Rudolph
A very early purple-sprouting variety that starts to produce its large, tasty spears from midwinter.

Trixie AGM
A high yield of deep green, domed heads borne on compact, clubroot-resistant plants.

Brussels sprouts

It is said that Brussels sprouts were developed in Belgium during the 13th century. Each sprout is a perfect little cabbage growing in whorls around tall stems that can grow up to 1m (3½ft) high. They have a nutty, often peppery taste and you either love or hate them. Perhaps the person who developed them loved cabbage but couldn't eat very much at one sitting.

In our house everyone apart from my husband, Neil, says they dislike them, but at Christmas we always cook a lot because the moment they are spotted everyone wants great heaps of them. And by preparing a lot there will always be some for a Boxing Day 'bubble and squeak'. Surprisingly, there are few recipes for sprouts, although they can

often be substituted for cabbage. Try adding them to pasta with toasted walnuts, or sautéed, adding lemon juice and thyme.

Sprouts take little time to prepare and cook. The cooking method that suits them least is the one they get most often which produces a soggy, tasteless heap. Boiling them to death slowly is the worst way: they should be steamed or boiled fast and briefly to retain their nutty taste and crunch. Making a cross with a sharp knife in the base of the sprout with a sharp knife speeds up cooking time.

Recent breeding of sweeter cultivars means people have even started eating them as a raw vegetable. Cored and cut finely, and dressed with toasted pine nuts and a good vinaigrette with plenty of mustard, they go brilliantly with Stilton or any robust cheese. But to eat good sprouts you must first grow them, and grow them well. They prefer slightly alkaline, deep soil, an open position and firm planting. Sprouts are particularly vulnerable to wind damage because they are so tall and top-heavy. If plants rock around in the wind, the roots get damaged and the sprouts will blow open up and fail to make those lovely little solid buttons.

Most of us need just a few plants. Since they will be harvested a few at a time from the bottom of the stem up, a few plants should last a couple of months. The magnificent plants make an eye-catching addition to the winter vegetable garden. The purple-leaved varieties are even more striking.

BRUSSELS SPROUTS are tight 'axillary buds' that form in the leaf axils of the plants. The looser 'terminal bud' at the growing tips of plants makes tasty greens.

Brussels sprouts

Brassica oleracea (Gemmifera Group)

Brussels sprouts are a delicacy when cooked fresh from the garden. The sprouts stay ready to pick on their stems for some time, and can be picked over a three-month period. By carefully selecting the right varieties, it is possible to enjoy fresh Brussels sprouts from early autumn until spring, but frost really does bring out the best in them.

	J	F	M	A	M	J	J	A	S	O	N	D
Sow			.	.	.							
Plant				.	.	.	.					
Harvest	.	.	.						.	.	.	.

The best sites and soils

For a good crop of Brussels sprouts ideally you need a firm soil with a pH of 6–7.5, but they really aren't too fussy. Choose a sunny site with shelter from high winds to avoid the risk of this top-heavy crop being blown over. If in doubt, support plants with a 5 x 2.5cm (2 x 1in) stake to keep them upright.

Prepare the soil by digging in generous quantities of organic matter such as well-rotted manure or garden compost, during autumn. This advance preparation helps ensure that the soil has consolidated by planting time. Avoid digging over the soil shortly before planting.

Sowing and planting

Young plants are easily raised from seed, either in seedbeds or modules (see page 70) from early to mid-spring. Prepare a firm seedbed and sow as for broccoli (see pages 74 and 75).

The seedlings should appear within 7–12 days, when they can be thinned out so that they are 7.5cm (3in) apart. Transplant the seedlings in mid-spring to early summer when they are roughly 10–15cm (4–6in) high. If the seedlings have been grown in modules, transplant them when the roots begin to show through the bottom of the tray.

Allow 76cm (30in) between the plants and the rows. Resist the temptation to squeeze in more plants, because the distance makes picking easier and the

WHEN TRANSPLANTING the seedlings, make sure that you allow enough space around them for air to circulate over the leaves as this will help to prevent fungal diseases.

improved air circulation will help to prevent fungal diseases. Plant the seedlings so that the soil is level with the first set of true leaves, and water as for broccoli (see page 74).

Cultivating the crop

Water the crop regularly while it is establishing, and during dry spells. Also reduce competition for moisture and nutrients by regularly hoeing off weeds around the plants. Sprinkle nitrogen-rich fertilizer around plants that are not growing well.

At harvest time

The first, early varieties of Brussels sprouts are ready from early autumn, although many gardeners wait until after the first hard frosts, which make sprouts taste sweeter. Select only firm sprouts, which should be about the size of a walnut, and snap them off or remove with a sharp knife. Start from the bottom and work up, removing a few from each plant at a time. Also remove and discard any yellowing leaves. Once the entire stem has been cleared, the leafy top can be harvested and cooked like cabbage.

Storing and cooking tips

Since Brussels sprouts do not store well, it is best to leave them on the plant and pick as required. If there's a glut, firm, healthy sprouts can be frozen, but avoid overcooking after freezing: they require only a brief boiling or they become too soft. Freshly harvested sprouts should also be lightly cooked to obtain maximum crispness, flavour and colour. They have a high nutritional value, and are full of antioxidants and vitamin C.

Pests and diseases

Protect Brussels sprouts from some of the more damaging insects with a net. Cabbage whitefly and Aphids can be especially difficult to control. Use a physical-action insecticide if infestations are severe.

YOUNG BRUSSELS SPROUTS plants should be supported with a stake to ensure that they grow upright.

Recommended varieties

Revenge AGM
A high-yielding variety with firm sprouts from mid- to late winter.

Red Delicious
An unusual and ornamental red variety to try that stays purple on cooking. The sprouts are ready to pick from late autumn. They lack the vigour of the other varieties.

Cumulus
A strong-growing, adaptable variety with dark green sprouts on tall plants. Good disease resistance.

Maximus AGM
High yields of round, smooth, medium-sized mid-green buttons from autumn on. Powdery mildew tolerant.

Cabbages

Cabbage is much maligned. In fact it has probably had the worst press of any vegetable. Most of us have had it at school, boiled to disintegration and unrecognizable save for its pungent smell, but it is one of the most widely grown of all vegetables and has been in cultivation since the earliest times.

Many gardeners resent growing cabbages because they take up a lot of space – but think about it. Cabbages are totally hardy, and can face cold and exposure and still be enormously productive. They come in every hue of green and purple, with textures ranging from smooth and tightly layered to open and crunchy with wonderfully puckered leaves. They can be spherical, pointed, or open and flat. And you can grow them for picking in every season. In the kitchen, cabbage can be double-cooked and fermented, as in sauerkraut, or thinly sliced and mixed with other raw vegetables for making coleslaw. It can be steamed briefly, or gently stewed with finely chopped garlic and onions and juniper berries (my favourite), or boiled with potatoes in the depths of winter.

Beginners think that growing cabbage is difficult, but that's not so. And if you have limited space then just choose your favourite cabbage, not least because it'll look impressive. Red cabbage takes a long time to mature, but it is versatile and beautiful. A big earthenware pot full of red cabbage layered with onions and Bramley apples and cooked with spices, wine vinegar and brown sugar is a rich and sumptuous dish.

AS YOU WATCH young cabbages form hearts, you will warm to them and may even begin to treat them as individuals!

Cabbages

Brassica oleracea (Capitata Group)

Rather undeservedly, cabbages have a reputation for being uninteresting, but once you start to grow your own you will see them as nothing of the sort. The different sizes, shapes and colours are a joy to behold, and they will feed you all year round. In the kitchen, you can use them raw in salad or coleslaw, as ingredients in soup, boiled or steamed in the traditional way, or lightly braised.

Spring Cabbage

	J	F	M	A	M	J	J	A	S	O	N	D
Sow							•	•				
Plant									•	•		
Harvest				•	•							

Summer Cabbage

	J	F	M	A	M	J	J	A	S	O	N	D
Sow	•	•	•	•								
Plant					•	•						
Harvest							•	•	•	•	•	

Autumn Cabbage

	J	F	M	A	M	J	J	A	S	O	N	D
Sow			•	•	•							
Plant					•	•						
Harvest									•	•	•	

Winter Cabbage

	J	F	M	A	M	J	J	A	S	O	N	D
Sow					•	•						
Plant						•	•					
Harvest	•	•	•								•	•

Different types of cabbage

Cabbages are grouped by season of interest – spring, summer, autumn and winter. Hybrids between the types have produced some attractive and tasty cabbages. It is possible to grow cabbages in containers if space is limited, or if your soil conditions are not appropriate.

Spring cabbages grow over the winter and give small, pointed cabbages or spring greens at the time of year when not much else is available.

Summer and autumn cabbages include varieties that cope well with hot summer conditions, as well as the red cabbages, some of which can be treated as winter cabbages since they are suitable for lifting and storing over winter.

Winter cabbages include some quite ornamental varieties, useful for livening up the bare winter garden. They range from smooth, globular

SOWING CABBAGE SEED

1 EVENLY SPRINKLE a good number of seeds across a whole tray of compost. Allow a finger width between each seed.

2 COVER THE SEEDS with a thin layer of seed compost and then gently firm this down by hand or using the bottom of another seed tray.

3 WATER THE COMPOST carefully so that it is evenly soaked. Leave the seeds to germinate in a sunny place. Keep the compost moist.

drumheads to crinkle-leaved semi-Savoy types, to hardy Savoys with their heavily textured leaves, which can be harvested through the coldest months. There are also white- and purple-tinged varieties, like 'January King', and some are suitable for lifting and storing.

The best sites and soils

To produce sound, large heads of crispy leaves, cabbages need a sunny site and firm soil. Dig in well-rotted organic matter in autumn to give the soil time to consolidate over winter. Also check the soil pH, as the ideal range is 6–7.5, but cabbages really aren't that fussy; if it is too low, you may need to apply lime, which will help to deter the disease clubroot. Before planting, firm up the soil in spring as explained on page 70. Before planting or sowing summer or autumn cabbages, apply a general fertilizer at the manufacturer's recommended dose.

Sowing and planting

All four groups of cabbage are grown in exactly the same way, but the sowing times vary. Sow summer cabbages from late winter to late spring and autumn cabbages from early to late spring; red cabbages need an early spring sowing as they are slow growers. Successive sowings over a number of weeks provide a gradual harvest, avoiding a sudden glut. Winter cabbages need to be sown when winter is the last thing on your mind, during the arrival of summer. Spring cabbages can be sown from mid- to late summer for cropping the following year. Cabbages can either be sown into a prepared seedbed outdoors (as for broccoli, see page 74), into seed trays or modules for later planting, or sown directly where they are to grow (see pages 70–71). If sown in a seedbed, the young cabbages will be later transplanted to their final positions. Thoroughly prepare the soil before sowing directly outdoors by raking the surface to create a fine, crumbly texture.

Recommended varieties (spring)

Duncan AGM
Useful for both spring and summer harvest, bears a plentiful crop of small, pointed mid- to dark green heads.

Wheeler's Imperial
A compact dwarf variety, good if space is tight. As well as for late spring greens, it will also grow as an autumn cabbage.

Recommended varieties (summer)

Hispi AGM
An early summer cabbage producing medium-sized, pointed heads with excellent flavour. Stays in good condition in the garden for a long period without splitting.

Kilaxy
Has been hailed as a breeding breakthrough because of its clubroot resistance, and has tasty, firm and compact heads ready from late summer to autumn.

AVOIDING SPLIT HEADS

Cabbage hearts can be prone to splitting when watered irregularly, so it is essential to ensure that the plants have an adequate and regular supply. Frost can also cause splitting, so choose hardy varieties. Overmaturity also leads to splitting. A folk remedy is to twist the plants when mature to stop growth and therefore prevent splitting.

Stretch a length of string as a guide, and draw out a straight 1cm (½in) deep drill by dragging a measuring rod, hoe or broom handle along the line. If the bottom of the drill is dry, lightly water first. Sprinkle the seed thinly along its length, and cover with soil, which should be gently firmed by lightly patting down. Seedlings usually appear after 7–12 days. Thin out to the strongest, leaving them 7.5cm (3in) apart, and weed regularly. All cabbage seedlings need to be given protection from cabbage root fly by placing collars around their stems. Cover seedbeds with fleece or insect-proof netting.

Unless the seeds were direct-sown where they are to grow, plant out the young cabbage plants into prepared, firmed soil by early summer for summer and autumn cabbages, by midsummer for winter cabbages, and during autumn for spring cabbages. Plant as for broccoli (see page 74).

Allow 30–45cm (12–18in) between the plants and rows, depending on the size of the variety. Specific planting advice should be provided on the seed packet. Spring cabbages can be grown more closely, at 10cm (4in) apart, in rows 30cm (12in) apart. Alternate ones can be taken early for use in the kitchen as spring greens, which help to thin the crop out. The remaining spring cabbages should be left to mature in the ground for a later harvest.

Cultivating the crop

Cabbages are robust if 'puddled in' (see page 70), needing little water. In prolonged dry spells, a thorough soak every ten days will be enough. When hearts begin to form, generous watering will greatly improve head size; just one watering can make all the difference.

Recommended varieties (winter)

Protovoy AGM
A very early, well-blistered, small Savoy cabbage with dark green outer leaves and paler, solid hearts.

Tundra AGM
Ready from late autumn onwards, a Savoy cabbage with attractive dark green heads of firm, sweet-tasting leaves that last all winter in the ground.

Pixie AGM
Sometimes grown as a spring cabbage for its late winter and early spring crop of small, well-hearted heads of mid-green leaves.

January King 3
A hardy drumhead cabbage with attractively red-tinged leaves. It matures from late autumn and stands well over winter.

RED CABBAGE grows slowly, but is especially delicious. It is prone to damage by low winter temperatures, but some varieties can be lifted and stored over winter.

To provide additional protection from both wind and frost, you should pile up some soil around the base of each plant before the first heavy frosts. This protects the stem of the plant and is known as 'earthing up'.

To prevent any kind of rot, it is good practice to remove dead leaves when they appear. Summer, autumn and winter cabbages can be given a feed containing fertilizer with a high-nitrogen content before they get too big, and spring cabbages should be fed in early spring.

At harvest time

Cut off the plants close to the ground with a sharp knife, or remove young leaves as and when they are needed. After harvesting the first spring and early summer cabbages, cut a cross in the top of the stump, about 1cm (½in) deep, and the plant will produce a cluster of smaller heads within about five weeks.

Most cabbages can be harvested as required, with many winter varieties being tough enough to last outdoors through the whole winter. Those that are prone to winter damage, such as red, white and some green cabbages, should be harvested and stored before the first frosts.

Storing and cooking tips

Cabbage is extremely good for you, being full of antioxidants and a source of vitamin C. Spring, summer and autumn cabbages are best eaten when freshly harvested, but some red and white cabbages, if large enough, can be lifted in autumn for storage. Remove some of the outer leaves, and then store in straw-lined boxes in a cool, dry place where they will last until early spring. Inspect the heads periodically for signs of rotting and gently remove any withered leaves, taking care not to bruise the head. Alternatively, you could leave them in the ground and harvest them as and when they are needed.

Many varieties can be used in stir-fries or turned into delicious home-made coleslaw. Red cabbage is also excellent at Christmas when combined with apple. To retain the red colour when cooking, add vinegar to the water. White cabbages are used in coleslaw and other salads. Whole heads of cabbages and large leaves rolled up can be stuffed and baked.

WINTER CABBAGES have immense value as they stand through the leanest months of the year, waiting to be picked for the table.

Cauliflowers
Brassica oleracea (Botrytis Group)

Cauliflowers have a reputation for being rather tricky to grow but, for many gardeners, that's the challenge. They certainly need attention, and are the most sensitive members of the cabbage family to the pH of the soil, but a little time spent on soil preparation, followed by plenty of watering through the growing season, can achieve excellent results.

	J	F	M	A	M	J	J	A	S	O	N	D
Sow	■			■	■					■	■	■
Plant			■	■	■	■	■	■				
Harvest	■	■	■		■	■	■	■	■	■	■	■

Different types of cauliflower

True cauliflowers have creamy white heads, or curds, but there are hybrids with purple, lime-green and even orange heads. Cauliflowers can be grown all year round, although the 'Roscoff' varieties, for harvesting from early to mid-winter, can be reliably grown only in very mild areas. Most winter varieties mature in spring, taking up space for a long time.

If you can't devote large areas of the garden to cauliflowers for a lengthy period, try the fast-maturing miniature summer varieties which can be sown close together from early spring for a high yield. The standard-size summer varieties are ready to harvest in as little as three months from a spring sowing. And the autumn varieties, sown in summer, are ready to harvest from early to late autumn and range from large-headed varieties to the more compact Australian-bred types.

The best sites and soils

Cauliflowers require a sunny site with deep, firm, moisture-retentive soil. Dig in plenty of manure to improve the soil's moisture-holding capacity in autumn, so that it has plenty of time to settle and consolidate over winter. Early digging also avoids poorly formed curds. Check that the soil has a pH of 6.5–7.5. Rotate your crops to reduce the likelihood of clubroot and other potential problems. Never grow cauliflowers in the same position within two years.

Sowing and planting

Summer varieties can be sown in mid-autumn in a cold frame, or in mid-winter in the glasshouse at 10–16°C (50–60°F). In both cases the seed can be sown in pots, and the young plants then hardened off ready for planting out from early spring for harvesting in early summer. Alternatively, sow the seed of all varieties outside from mid- to late spring. Either sow the seed directly where it is to grow (thinning to final required spacing), raise the crop in a seedbed for transplanting later, or germinate seed in modules (see page 70). For direct sowing, mark out a row with string and form the drill with a tool handle or measuring stick (see page 72).

HARVEST CAULIFLOWERS while the heads are still firm and small, and before the curds have started to separate, to ensure that the crop lasts for a longer period.

Cultivating the crop

Transplant seedbed-raised seedlings as soon as they are large enough to handle, ideally at around six weeks old. Water them shortly before you begin. Replant the seedlings 60cm (24in) apart, but leave 75cm (30in) between the slow-maturing winter varieties. Transplant winter types from mid- to late summer to avoid leaves forming among the curds.

Ensure that the soil is kept moist at all times through the growing season. To prevent the curds being discoloured by direct sunlight, or by a severe frost followed by a rapid thaw, bend one of the uppermost leaves over the developing curd to protect it. Many modern varieties are extremely hardy and will withstand severe winter weather, so are ideal in very cold districts. Cold weather may cause browning of the curds and leaves, although this can also be caused by boron deficiency, which is treated by regularly applying a foliar feed.

Harvesting

Begin cutting the heads while they are still small – before the curds start to separate – so that the crop can be enjoyed over a longer period as it gradually develops. It should be harvested by cutting through the stem with a sharp knife. Leave some of the leaves intact around the head to protect it from damage during handling and storage.

Storing and cooking tips

Cauliflower is best used straight away, but can be stored by being hung upside down by the stem in a cool, airy place. Spray the leaves regularly with water and it should keep for several weeks. It also freezes well, which might be a better way of maintaining supplies because it can be tricky to grow during the hot summer months or depths of winter.

Cauliflower is low in calories and packed with vitamin C. Overcooking can easily destroy the nutritional value as well as the delicate taste. The best way to appreciate cauliflower's flavour is to boil a shallow pan of water, add a squeeze of lemon juice, then carefully add the florets head-up and let them steam gently for about ten minutes. Lemon juice also helps retain the hues of colour varieties when they are cooked. Raw florets of coloured varieties make an attractive addition to salads.

Recommended varieties

Gypsy AGM
This variety produces large heads of clean white curds in summer, even on less fertile soils.

Igloo
A versatile early variety that can be grown closely spaced for a quick crop of small heads. Crops in midsummer.

Lateman
The late harvesting period of this cauliflower, from late summer into autumn, makes it useful for extending the season.

Graffiti AGM
Solid curds of a good size with a very attractive amethyst colour, which is best retained if steamed rather than boiled. They are also very tasty raw in salads.

Kale

" A close relation of cabbage, kale shares lots of family characteristics but has a distinctive personality of its own. Aesthetically it far surpasses its cabbage cousins. The leaves are so ornamental that many are used in a purely decorative capacity in the garden. They are separated from each other, and often heavily serrated or fringed around their margins. Many, such as black Tuscan 'Cavolo Nero', have deeply crinkled leaves of rich sea-green, held upright in a striking, architectural pose. Some, like 'Red Sails', are positively frilly and, when combined with such an opulent colour, more attractive than all other vegetables and most ornamental plants. When the plant is full-grown the purple stems develop a velvety bloom. It's a small wonder that kale is the most photographed garden vegetable.

Kale is often thought of as a lowly vegetable, more suitable for animals than humans, but that's wrong. It is tasty and robust, full of vitamins A and C, and packed with minerals. And because of the extreme hardiness of most varieties, it is available when it is needed most: in late autumn and winter. The flavour develops as the leaves mature, and frost improves it even further.

These winter leaves can be harvested from late autumn to early spring, and an earlier harvest can be taken from plants sown in March. The tender young leaves from this earlier crop are delicious in salads or cooked briefly with oil and garlic. A second sowing of kale in late spring or early summer will keep the harvest going for at least six months. Because only a few leaves are cut at a time, unlike cabbage or cauliflower where the whole head is harvested, kale really earns its keep.

With a little imagination the leaves can be turned into the most scrumptious food. Cut the mature leaves across the leaf in fine slices, deep fry for a maximum of one minute and sprinkle with a mixture of salt and sugar to make Chinese 'seaweed'. The older the leaves, the longer they may need cooking, but they retain their flavour and substance even when added to soups such as caldo verde, or green broth – a delicious Portuguese concoction that also contains potatoes, salt and water.

If space is limited, grow a few plants in the flower borders or as part of a winter container scheme. If you are gardening in a cold part of the country, remember that kale is immensely tough. No wonder it has been at the heart of many cottage garden vegetable plots for centuries. "

KALE is an excellent plant for the kitchen garden. Its tasty, nutritious leaves can be picked as needed through the winter.

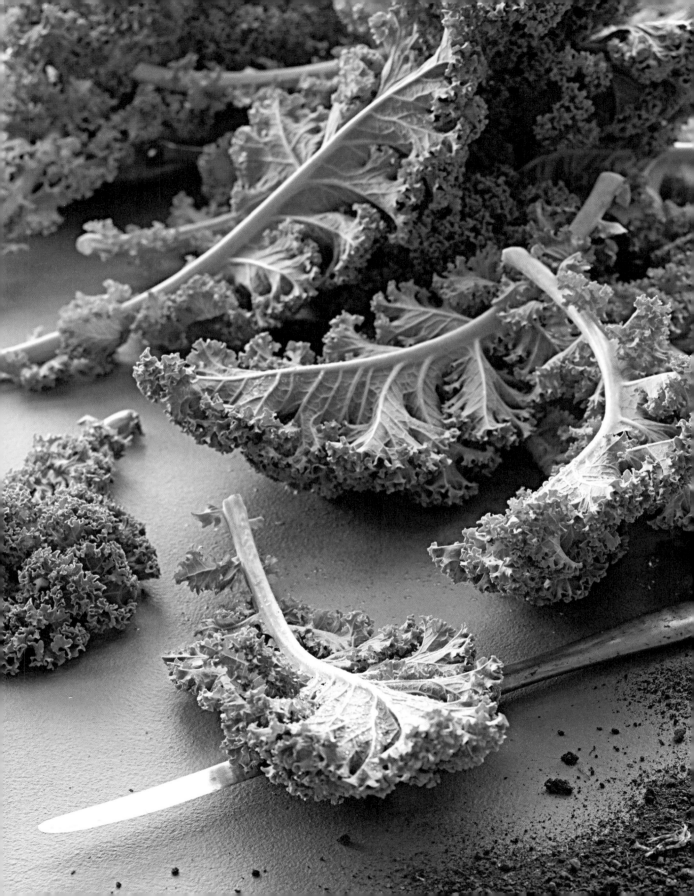

Kale
Brassica oleracea (Acephala Group)

Kale (Scotch kale or, more commonly, borecole) might not be familiar, but it has been grown for centuries. It is tasty, nutritious, and a rich source of iron and vitamins A, C and E. It is also very easy to grow. Some of the old-fashioned varieties had slightly bitter leaves, but new breeding – crossing curly kale with its flat-leaved counterparts – has produced a much more palatable vegetable.

	J	F	M	A	M	J	J	A	S	O	N	D
Sow					▪	▪	▪					
Plant						▪	▪	▪				
Harvest	▪	▪	▪	▪	▪				▪	▪	▪	▪

Different types of kale

There are four main groups of kale: curly-leaved, plain-leaved, rape kale, and the leaf and spear varieties.Their crinkly, usually dark green, bluish-green or even bronze leaves form a cascade at the top of a stout, often tall, stem. Plants are grown in flower borders for their attractive leaves, and used in winter as decorative 'ornamental cabbages'.

The best sites and soils

Kale has many advantages over other brassicas. It tolerates a little shade, is completely frost-hardy, and is not so vulnerable to the pests and diseases that afflict the others. It can also be grown in virtually any soils, including impoverished, wet, loose and poor ones. However, adding well-rotted organic matter, such as manure or garden compost, or hoeing a granular fertilizer such as pelleted chicken manure into the soil surface, will improve the crop.

Sowing and planting

To raise kale the traditional way, in seedbeds for winter and spring greens, sow from mid- to late spring. Rape kale dislikes being transplanted, so sow in the ground in early summer for a harvest the following spring. Seeds can be sown in modules (see page 70). For all types, thoroughly prepare the soil before sowing by raking the surface to create a fine crumbly texture. Use a length of string as a guide and make a 1cm (½in) drill (see page 74). The seedlings should appear within 7–12 days. Dwarf and standard height varieties are available. The advantage of growing dwarf types is that you can cram more crops into the space, and they also work well as cut-and-come-again crops (see box). Tall varieties are more commonplace.

Cultivating the crop

Transplant young kale to its final position 6–8 weeks after sowing. Water the the plants thoroughly before moving, and 'puddle in' plants (see page 70) once they are in their final position. The seedlings should be set 45cm (18in) apart, and planted firmly to the depth of the first set of true leaves. Keep the plants watered during dry spells. Support stems firmly using a stout wooden stake. Remove any yellowing leaves.

Harvesting

Kale is completely frost-hardy, and young leaves can be picked and enjoyed from autumn to mid-spring.

CUT-AND-COME-AGAIN

Kale can also be grown as a ground-hugging, cut-and-come-again crop. This involves trimming off the tender young leaves to encourage more to form, so keeping the plants bushy and compact. This is an attractive, productive way to grow kale, particularly when using the purple-leaved varieties. Sow the seed where you want it to grow, either in blocks or in bands threaded through other plants, and harvest when the kale is about 5cm (2in) high. It will soon grow more leaves which can either be cut again or be allowed to mature into a shorter, bushier plant.

PLANTS WILL BE READY to harvest from late autumn to mid-spring. Remove them when their leaves are still young and tender and this will encourage more side shoots to grow.

Varieties of rape kale are best enjoyed from early to late spring. Harvest all types while the leaves are still young and tender; older leaves quickly become tough and bitter. Start from the crown of the plant and work outwards, removing the tips of the stems with a sharp knife. This will encourage the plant to bush out and produce more side shoots.

Storing and cooking tips

Harvest the crop as required because it will stay fresh in the refrigerator for only a few days. The spring leaves can be frozen for use later in the year and many varieties bear broccoli-like spears at this time.

KEEP PLANTS HEALTHY by hoeing weeds from underneath them and removing dead leaves from the lower stems, which helps to ensure good air circulation.

When grown as a cut-and-come-again crop, kale is extremely tender and can be added to salads and stir-fries. Kale has a strong flavour which resembles spinach and cabbage, but doesn't have the tough, chewy leaf veins. It is usually boiled, but steaming or stir-frying retains more of the flavour and goodness.

Recommended varieties

Dwarf Green Curled
Grows to 60cm (24in) high unless grown as a cut-and-come-again crop, and has dark, tightly curled leaves all winter, keeping them well into spring.

Bornick AGM
The finely curled, mid-green leaves are excellent for early cropping as they mature quickly. Good pest and disease resistance.

Redbor AGM
A beautiful, jewel-like purple which looks fabulous with the blue-green of leeks. A must for the potager, and in ornamental beds and borders.

Fribor AGM
A very hardy variety with densely frilly-edged, dark green leaves. Good pest and disease resistance.

Beans and peas

Peas and beans, commonly known as legumes are delicious and decorative as both pods and seed. Peas have translucent pods that hang down revealing their embryonic treasure, and runner beans were grown first for their flowers, pretty white or pink petals scattered along branching stems, when they were introduced to Europe from the New World. It's easy to understand how the seeds became currency. Besides this, legumes leave nitrogen in the soil, maintaining its fertility, and their tops – often quite extensive in the case of runner beans – are a real bonus on the compost heap.

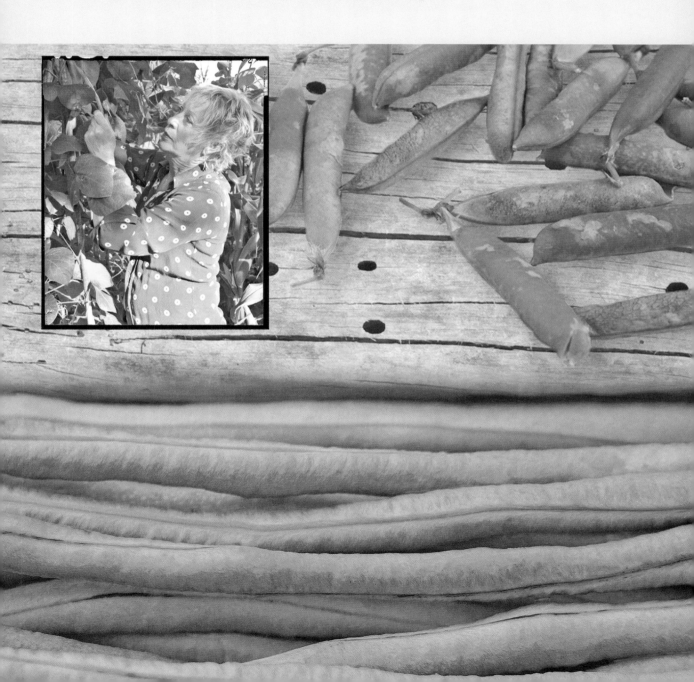

Broad beans

" Broad beans are beans for beginners. Anyone can grow them, their only requirements being decent soil, good light, and water. In the legume plot, they are the first crop to be sown and, where the soil is well-drained and stays reasonably warm over winter, they can even be sown in autumn. With luck they'll be ready to pick in late spring.

As with peas, you eat the seed. The beans can be eaten raw or cooked, fresh or dried, and can be stored over winter. Their texture is rich and thick, and their taste floury and satisfying. Excavated Stone Age settlements have yielded cultivated broad beans from at least 3000 BC, and they were grown right across Europe, including the Mediterranean and the Iberian peninsula. Both the black beans and the pale beans we use today were known and grown in ancient horticulture.

Because of their 'storeability', they were highly prized and put to a number of uses. In the Roman senate, black beans denoted a 'No' vote, pale ones a 'Yes'. In China they are recent newcomers, appearing there only from AD 1200, but the Chinese now grow more beans than anyone else. They were probably transported there via The Silk Route. The Spanish introduced them to Central and South America at the same time, bringing runner beans and French beans to Europe. Vegetables have made some astonishing journeys around the globe and, in many cases, have been subsumed into a new culture, becoming as familiar as traditional food.

Like other legumes, broad beans make handsome plants, although taller varieties may need some support to stop them looking ungainly. They are strong, eager plants with attractive, often glaucous foliage borne in whorls around the stems. The dense clusters of flowers, white with a chocolate splodge, are sweetly scented to attract pollinators. A few heritage varieties have deep pink flowers. As they fade, the tiny pods begin to grow, eventually swelling to fat, waxy pods, shiny and robust.

They should be picked successionally, just before they reach maturity. The beans are eaten young and fresh when the pod is tight with its cargo, but before it reaches bursting point. Podding broad beans is a sensual delight, the hard, shiny exterior casing contrasting with the furry interiors that enclose the beans. For storing, place the picked beans in a dry place until they are completely dry, then put them in an air-tight tin or waxed paper bag. If they can survive from the Stone Age, they'll cope in the kitchen cupboard. Like all beans, they are rich in protein and high in riboflavin and vitamin C. "

BROAD BEAN PODS will be ready in late spring or early summer when the pods are full and fresh.

Broad beans *Vicia faba*

Versatile broad beans can produce a huge crop, they are fun to pick, and they are absolutely delicious. They are not hard to grow either, with large seeds that you can plunge directly into the soil. All you have to do is mind the weeds. A winter sowing will give an early summer harvest that can be cleared away immediately and planted with the next summer crop.

	J	F	M	A	M	J	J	A	S	O	N	D
Sow	■	■	■							■	■	■
Plant			■	■	■							
Harvest				■	■	■	■					

The best sites and soils

Broad beans need a sunny, sheltered site because mature plants, when bushy and weighted with pods, are liable to wind damage. They are less fussy about their soil requirements than peas or French beans, but still benefit from well-rotted organic matter being dug in the ground before planting.

Sowing and planting

If you want an early crop of beans, sow the seed outdoors the previous autumn, provided the soil is still warm. Choose a hardy variety.

Alternatively, sow seed outside from early spring on, depending on the weather. If the soil temperature is low, warm it by covering with polythene to aid germination. You could also sow the seed under cover, one per root trainer or small pot, taking care to

SOWING BEANS in seed modules is a little more high-maintenance than direct sowing, but it ensures successful early sowings.

acclimatize the seedlings to life outside before planting them out.

Broad beans are prolific croppers once they get going, so aim for a series of small successional sowings of

Recommended varieties

The Sutton AGM
Dwarf variety and prolific cropper, excellent for exposed sites, containers raised beds and small gardens.

Aquadulce Claudia AGM
You can sow seed outdoors in mid-autumn or even late autumn, provided the soil is still warm. Hardy and early maturing.

8–12 seeds, with a few substitutes in case of failures. Using a trowel or dibber, sow seeds individually at a depth of 5cm (2in). Seeds should be 23cm (9in) apart, either in double rows or in small blocks, but in either case make sure that the rows are staggered to maximise the spaces between.

Successional sowings

Broad beans take about nine to ten weeks to mature, which means that between early and late spring you should be able to manage another one or two sowings to ensure a more prolonged, even harvest. There is no set time for a second or third sowing; just wait until the previous one has reached a height of about 15-20cm (6–8in) before sowing the next crop. Do not be tempted to sow more plants before this, however, or the second sowing will probably catch up with the first.

If you have autumn-sown beans, delay your first spring sowing until the weather is warm enough for the autumn beans to have put on some strong new growth.

Supporting the plants

Plants in exposed sites will fall over in the wind or lose stems under the weight of the swelling pods unless they are staked. Old, long, strong and twiggy prunings can be used to create an unobtrusive network of support; put these in place once the seedlings have emerged. Alternatively, plants can be tied to structures made from string roped around a series of stakes or strong bamboo canes.

Cultivating the crop

When the young beans begin to appear at the base of the plant, it is time to 'pinch out' the growing tips in order to concentrate the beans' energy on pod formation. Nip off the top of the stem with two pairs of leaves attached; these can be eaten.

At harvest time

Harvest beans when they are small, before the flesh becomes starchy and the skin bitter. Take pods from the base of the plant and work up. Because it can be easy to damage plants while picking pods, it is best to use scissors or secateurs to snip them off.

HARVESTING BROAD BEANS

1 START TO PICK broad beans, using scissors or secateurs, when the pods are full but still fresh.

2 REMOVE THE MORE MATURE pods from the bottom of the plant first. The beans should be a good size and firm to the touch.

Storing and cooking tips

Broad beans freeze well, but need to be blanched first. Don't dispose of the thinning tips; they are are delicious to eat wilted in pasta or risotto dishes.

Pests and diseases

Black bean aphids can be quite a pest. They often colonize the young shoots first, where they find it easy to suck the sap. Insecticides with a physical means of action should be used only if infestations are severe, and they do minimal harm to helpful insects. If you do see aphids, immediately pinch out the tips with finger and thumb. Planting herbs to repel or distract aphids is more wishful thinking than anything else.

In early spring, pea and bean weevils are active, eating semi-circular notches into leaf edges. Plants are unlikely to be seriously damaged by this, except in very poor weather when new leaf growth is slow. Covering with fleece is the best remedy.

Two common fungal diseases are chocolate spot and rust, visible as brown or orange spots on the leaves. Chocolate spot tends to occur in damp, humid weather early in the season, and rust during dry spells later on. Neither is usually severe so they are not worth treating.

French beans

" French beans are a more refined crop than runner beans. They need careful nurturing at first, and though they're not as productive as their cousins, their texture and taste more than make up for it.

In cold summers, French beans often get off to a slow start, but in a hot summer they cope better than runners. Unless you have perfect conditions – warm, fertile and completely slug-free – it's probably best to grow plants in pots, under glass or on a kitchen windowsill, and stand them out once they are established, and when the frosts are over.

Putting one or two beans into a biodegradable pot is ideal – or sow them in modules or cell trays and transplant them later into bigger pots, allowing them to develop adult leaves and a really strong root system before they are planted out. I tried direct sowing and, although a few survived, they were not a patch on those given a sheltered start.

There are broadly two types of French beans, the dwarf bush types and the climbers. If you have room for an obelisk or bamboo wigwam, the sight of bunches of slender climbing beans

FRENCH BEANS trained up cane structures can be an attractive feature of any vegetable garden.

hanging down is very rewarding. Although the flowers are usually fairly inconspicuous, the purple-podded varieties also have dark foliage and attractive purple flowers. Try growing them over an arch so that you can walk underneath and start picking. The real reason for growing French beans is their exquisite flavour. Steam them whole for a couple of minutes, then drizzle with oil.

In its natural habitat, the French bean is a forest climber, scrambling over shrubs and trees, and is found from Mexico, through Central America to Argentina. In Peru, seeds of cultivated plants have been found that date back to 6000 BC. It was later purloined by Europeans who took it back to try in their own gardens. The Huguenots introduced it to England, hence the name 'French' bean.

European hybridists have had a field day, no doubt making use of various forms of French beans from up and down Central and South America. Some have golden waxy pods, some are striped and speckled in crimson, others are slender and green. The white beans are rarely used in British cooking but are prominent in other cuisines. The French love haricots and flageolets, and borlotti are an Italian favourite.

French beans grow easily on most unimproved soils. If your soil is poor, however, regardless of whether you are growing climbing or dwarf varieties, dig out a decent trench and enrich it with well-rotted organic matter. Return the soil and, when it has settled and the frosts are over, put out your young plants and watch them go. "

French beans *Phaseolus vulgaris*

French beans are wonderful to eat and are ideal for the small garden. There are far more varieties than most people realise, and many are highly ornamental. As well as green beans, some are yellow, purple and cream and sometimes flecked. The young pods can be eaten whole or sliced, and the fresh 'haricot' beans within mature pods are also excellent.

	J	F	M	A	M	J	J	A	S	O	N	D
Sow				■	■		■	■				
Plant					■		■					
Harvest						■	■	■	■	■		

The best sites and soils

Like all legumes, French beans need a warm, sunny site with fertile soil that's moisture-retentive without being wet. Fork in some well-rotted manure or garden compost in late autumn or early winter.

Sowing and planting

All French beans are tender plants that will quickly succumb to a late frost. But even without frost, seedlings grow slowly and erratically in cool temperatures, making it difficult for them to shrug off attacks from slugs. It is far better to wait until late spring or early summer to sow, with two seeds per pot at 5cm (2in) deep; plant out once they are 8cm (3in) tall. Space plants 15–20cm (6–8in) apart, and always sow a few extras for possible gap fillers.

Dwarf beans are best grown in small blocks, where neighbouring plants provide support and some protection. Alternatively, sow in single or double rows using the same spacing.

The simplest, most traditional structure is a bamboo cane wigwam or double row of canes. The canes should be about 20cm (8in) apart, and a minimum of 1.8m (6ft) tall. Grow one plant per cane to avoid congestion. Climbing beans can also be trained up a trellis, over arches or along fences to make the most of their beautiful white or lilac flowers and ornamental pods. Whichever way you choose, they will usually need some initial encouragement to propel them in the right direction. Tie in young shoots because they can unwind from canes in windy weather.

Cultivating the crop

If you are caught out by a spell of unexpectedly cold weather after sowing, cover the plants with fleece until it is warmer. If you do not have fleece, cover them with newspaper overnight, especially if frost is

Recommended varieties

Kenyan bean AGM
This dwarf French bean produces slender, stringless 'Kenyan' bean pods. They are tender, easy to prepare and delicious.

Purple Teepee
A dwarf variety with beautiful purple pods. They turn green on cooking, with excellent flavour.

CLIMBING FRENCH BEANS, such as 'Algarve' (above), will need to be grown up a sturdy support. They make good, fast-growing screens.

PICK FRENCH BEANS once the plants start cropping in summer. The young pods will be sweetest, and regular picking will stimulate the growth of more beans.

forecast. Young seedlings are also prone to attacks from birds (especially pigeons and partridges), which can strip entire sowings. Windy weather is another problem, since it can desiccate or strip leaves, and damage any climbing stems that weren't tied in.

The best solution to both birds and wind is a supporting layer of twiggy brush around young plants, which will later prevent dwarf beans from flopping on the ground under the weight of the beans.

Mulching around the base of plants also helps minimize moisture loss. When climbing beans reach the top of their supports, pinch out the growing tips to prevent them becoming top-heavy.

At harvest time

Harvest pods as soon as they are large enough. Pods that snap crisply in half are at their peak. Harvest regularly to prolong cropping.

Storing and cooking tips

Young pods freeze well and mature beans can be dried. To dry beans, you should wait until the pods start to wither on the plants, then pick and lay them out in a dry, well-ventilated place to dry out before shelling and storing in an airtight container. Dry beans must be soaked before being cooked and eaten.

THE CHOICE: DWARF OR CLIMBING?

There are two main forms of French bean, dwarf and climbing. Dwarf beans grow into small, bushy plants about 45cm (18in) high, while climbing beans, like runner beans, will vigorously twine around anything they encounter up to a height of about 2–2.5m (6½–8ft). Dwarf beans are easier to maintain and pick but climbing beans, if cared for properly, produce many more beans in the same space.

Both beans produce clusters of pods on side shoots. Typically they are cylindrical and smooth-skinned, but some varieties are slightly flattened in shape, resembling a miniature runner bean. Some of the cylindrical beans are exceptionally slender and straight, and are often called filet beans or Kenyan types, after the country where most commercial production occurs. Besides the green varieties, purple- and yellow-podded and purple, freckled beans are also available. All look good on the plant, but the purple fades to deep green on cooking.

Some of the climbing beans produce broader, flat-podded beans that have a distinctive asymmetrical shape with one scalloped and one straight edge. They remain tender at quite a large size, and are particularly suitable for slicing into long, thin strips.

Runner beans

" If you want to grow a vegetable that will yield an enormous crop over a long period, look wonderful for months and take little effort, runner beans are the answer. There is something immensely satisfying about pushing a sleek, marbled pink seed into a pot of compost and a few days later seeing a robust green shoot impatient to grow, thrusting its way out of the dark compost. Then all you need do is provide a structure for the beans to grow up. Runner beans hoist themselves up any available vertical. They have such a lust for life – and boundless energy – that given sunshine, half-decent soil and enough to drink, they will reward you by flowering and fruiting endlessly.

Tall bamboo obelisks or stout hazel sticks make a perfect structure for their long twining stems and luscious green foliage spangled with vivid flowers. At the height of their growth they are big, heavy plants, so if you are in an area prone to strong winds, give them a protected position. In their natural habitat they grow high in the mountains protected by trees, which act as a climbing frame.

Pods must be continuously harvested to make the plants put out even more. Picking regularly, and this means every day, can ensure fresh young beans from mid-summer until mid-autumn. I always sow too many runner beans, and remember long ago having a double bean row with about 50 plants. It was a particularly cold, wet summer and the beans were put out when they were far too small. The slugs had a field day and we ended up with just three plants. But we still had a surplus. The moral is simple – don't grow too many.

Runner beans were brought here from Central America and Mexico in the 17th century as ornamental exotics because of their flowers. Only later were they exploited as vegetables. Picked when small, snapped and plunged into boiling water for a few minutes, they can be drained and eaten with butter or left to go cold for serving with a mild vinaigrette dressing. Either way – delicious. "

RUNNER BEANS are vigorous climbers with beautiful scarlet flowers. They will tower over most other crops on your vegetable patch.

Runner beans _Phaseolus coccineus_

Tall wigwams of runner beans are a classic feature of summer vegetable plots, and with their fast, lush growth and bright red flowers, they are sometimes seen in the ornamental garden too. They also tolerate a little bit of shade. Like all peas and beans, bacteria in the root nodules fix nitrogen into the soil from the air, which helps to maintain fertility levels in the soil.

	J	F	M	A	M	J	J	A	S	O	N	D
Sow					▪	▪	▪					
Plant					▪	▪						
Harvest							▪	▪	▪	▪	▪	

Different types of runner beans

French and runner beans are not dissimilar in their cultivation, but some people prefer the stronger taste and texture of runners. Although the tall climbers are most commonly grown, reaching up to 3m (10ft) in height, you can also get dwarf forms that would be good for growing under glass or if you do not have the space or inclination to construct a sturdy support.

Varieties with white or bicoloured flowers are available, although there is little difference in taste. The fresh speckled seeds are small objects of beauty.

The best sites and soils

Runner beans are not difficult to grow, but they are sensitive to frost, which is why they are grown as

RUNNER BEANS should be grown in a warm, sheltered position in the garden.

annuals and suit a warm, sheltered position. This also benefits pollinating insects, which are essential if the beans are to set their fruit. It is best to position these tall plants so that they do not shade the other plants in the vegetable plot. Construct a strong, well-secured support at least 1.8m (6ft) tall with canes 20cm (8in) apart.

You need to improve the soil before growing runner beans. A few months before planting, dig in plenty of well-rotted organic matter and add a general fertilizer before sowing.

Sowing and planting

Wait until mid- or late spring before sowing these seeds in pots indoors or on a windowsill. Sow two seeds per pot 5cm (2in) deep; they will soon germinate and can be planted out at the bottom of each upright support in early summer, 15cm (6in) apart, once the danger of late spring frosts has passed. The seedlings will soon wind their way onto the supports if you can give them a little direction; they grow at quite a rate, although they benefit from being loosely tied in at this stage.

For an early crop, sow seeds of a dwarf cultivar early in the year and grow them in a cloche or greenhouse. For a late crop in autumn, sow a batch of seeds in midsummer.

Watch out for slugs and snails, that will devour the seedlings if given half a chance, and mice, who may dig up and eat the seeds.

Cultivating the crop

Weed around the plants regularly, and water the plants in dry weather, particularly once the flowers begin to form. This helps with the development of

REMEMBER TO PINCH out the growing tips when they climb to the top of their support to prevent the beans becoming too top heavy.

bean pods. A thick mulch around the base of the plants is a good way of keeping the soil moist as well as keeping down weeds.

Pollinators may fail to do their job if the weather is too cold or windy, and this as well as inefficient irrigation is usually the cause of poor yields. Wetting foliage on warm evenings may cool the plants, improving pollination.

To prevent the beans becoming too top-heavy on their support, pinch out the growing tips when they reach the top.

At harvest time

It can take up to 12 weeks before you get your first crop of runner beans, but once they start coming, it is not easy to pick them fast enough. Pick beans while young before any hint of swelling seeds. Pods that are too old become stringy and are not worth eating; remove these unless you intend to save the seed to use next year.

By removing the old pods, it will stimulate the plant into further production. You can expect up to 1kg (2lb) of beans from a single plant.

Storing and cooking tips

Runner beans can have tough strings down both edges of the pod that need to be sliced off before the beans are sliced and then cooked. Beans picked young, however, will not have developed tough strings. Once sliced, the beans are ready to be frozen, or can be boiled or steamed right away for the table.

Recommended varieties

White Lady AGM
A top-quality variety with white flowers and high yields late into the season. The fleshy pods are smooth and stringless.

White Apollo AGM
The long, smooth fleshy pods crop prolifically over a long season and are of excellent quality. White flowers.

Carol's Veg Notebook

Peas

" Some legumes are grown for their pods. They are at their best before the seed starts to swell. With peas, however, we eat the seed and in some varieties, we also eat their pods.

There is something elemental about eating seed. It is the centre, the hub of the whole plant. From each one a whole new plant will grow. It's a plant in its most fundamental form. Nowadays they are produced in their billions for agriculture; bred to mature simultaneously to make the mass harvest as efficient as possible. We eat most of them frozen, and the rest are canned. Just compare that to picking and bursting open a pod and sampling the first few peas of the year... gardening doesn't get much better. The excitement of holding the fat green pod between thumb and forefinger and popping it open is magical.

When I was little, my mum used to tell me to shell the peas. Had she done it herself there would have been none left for tea, but because I didn't then like the taste of raw

RIPE PEA PODS in summer are irresistible. Pop them open between your thumb and forefinger and eat the peas fresh.

peas, there was no problem. Now I can't get enough of them. The best way to cook peas is quickly or you lose that delicious freshness. Possibly add a knob of mint-butter, and that's it. You don't need salt and pepper.

Sometimes, for an early crop, I sow my plants in short lengths of guttering (see Pests and Diseases, page 111) to steal a march on those sown in the ground. In my heavy clay, slugs, mice and cold wet conditions take their toll on early sowings. I like giving them a flying start so I get a quicker crop. Then I sow my peas in small blocks, with a week or a fortnight between each sowing. The aim is to avoid a glut, but if you get a run of hot weather they'll all ripen within a few days of each other. What do you do? Pick them all, make lots of soup, eat as many as you can, and freeze the rest.

Eating fresh peas is a recent development. Our ancestors used them as a winter staple: they keep well in a dry state losing little of their nutritional value, and provide next year's crop. Dried peas have turned up in archaeological sites from China, India and around the Nile to the Mediterranean and Europe. The Romans probably introduced them to Britain. They would have been ground as flour and mixed with grain flour to make bread, or soaked and cooked slowly for a nourishing meal. My mum used to make a wonderful warming winter soup with split peas, carrots, leeks and barley. Even when space is at a premium, you can grow one plant in a big pot, supported by twiggy sticks. "

Peas *Pisum sativum*

If you grow your own peas, don't be surprised if they never get as far as the kitchen. One of the many pleasures of having a vegetable patch is eating sweet, tender peas straight from the patch. The whole pod and its contents are eaten when you grow mangetout and sugarsnap peas, and they are delicious. Peas aren't keen on hot weather, so they make a good early summer crop.

	J	F	M	A	M	J	J	A	S	O	N	D
Sow			•	•	•	•	•					
Harvest						•	•	•	•	•	•	

Different types of peas

Peas are climbers with strong tendrils, and old varieties can reach heights of over 2m (6½ft). Although tall varieties are an effective way of using vertical space in a small garden, they require strong support. The quest for a self-supporting pea has led to much shorter cultivars, including dwarf varieties suitable for containers. Semi-leafless peas were bred for commercial crop production, being particularly well adapted for mechanical harvesting. As their name implies, they produce fewer leaves but more tendrils; grown in blocks, the plants can support one another without the crop becoming smothered by too much foliage.

Like potatoes, peas are grouped by the time taken to mature. Earlies take around 12 weeks, second earlies

PLANTING OUT SEEDLINGS

1 SOW EARLY PLANTS under cover in modules. This provides essential protection and is useful where pests such as mice are a problem.

2 PLANT PEA SEEDLINGS into the ground, when they are about 10cm (4in) tall. Insert supports around the plants. Remember to acclimatize the seedlings first.

13–14 weeks, and maincrops 15–16 weeks. The earlies can be sown throughout the summer.

When sowing different varieties of peas, you will notice that some seeds are wrinkled, whereas some are round. Generally, the latter are hardier and are used for very early sowings, but they lack the sweetness of wrinkled varieties, which are best for summer sowings.

Flat-podded mangetout peas are eaten pod and all, and are now widely available in supermarkets. The less-well-known sugar snap has a sweet and crunchy pod even when the peas have swelled, and is also eaten whole. Many of these varieties can also be used as shelling peas when left to develop. Peas described as petit pois remain small even when mature.

The best sites and soils

Peas like rich, moisture-retentive soil which has had additions of compost or well-rotted manure. Good soil preparation helps them through hot weather which they dislike, as does watering and then mulching around the base of the plant.

Sowing and planting

First sowing times outside vary according to location and weather. They are normally between early and mid-spring. Do not be tempted to sow into cold, wet ground because germination will be poor. If spring is slow to arrive, warm the soil by covering it with polythene before sowing, and then protect the seedlings with fleece. A traditional method of sowing peas, which works well with shorter varieties, is to make a flat trench, 5cm (2in) deep and about 25cm (10in) wide, with a hoe. Water the trench first, then sow the seeds 5–7cm (2–2¾in) apart in three rows along the bottom of the trench. Press the seed in a little so that it does not become displaced when the trench is backfilled with soil. Firm the ground lightly with the back of the hoe.

Both dwarf and semi-leafless varieties can also be sown in small blocks. Lay seed on the soil in an staggered pattern so that each is 13cm (6in) apart. If the soil is loose, simply push in the seed to a depth of 5cm (2in); otherwise use a trowel.

Sowing seed in a single row, or pair of rows, works best for taller varieties because it makes it easier to support them. It also gives increased air ventilation around the plants, helping to prevent powdery mildew as well as making weeding easier.

Make a single V-shaped drill, 5cm (2in) deep, water the base of the drill and sow the peas 5–10cm (2–4in) apart. You can add a second row, providing it is 30cm (12in) away, and insert supports between the two rows.

Successional sowing

In order to maintain a steady supply of peas through the season, there are two main strategies. Either sow an early variety every four weeks until midsummer, or make a single sowing of an early, second early, and maincrop variety, each of which will mature at different times.

Cultivating the crop

Put supports in place before the young plants become top-heavy and flop over. For dwarf and shorter

Recommended varieties (garden)

Early Onward
A reliable early variety with a high yield of blunt-ended pods that are carried in pairs.

Waverex
Excellent petit pois, with lots of small, sweetly flavoured peas. They are well-suited to freezing.

Recommended varieties (sugarsnap)

Sugar Ann AGM
The medium size of this sugarsnap pea will not need support. It bears a very early crop of succulent, sweet pods; older ones can be shelled.

Sugar Lord
A very tall, vigorous sugarsnap pea with an extremely high yield of tasty, brightly coloured pods.

Recommended varieties (mangetout)

Delikata AGM
A tall mangetout pea that is slightly earlier than 'Oregon Sugar Pod' and carries a heavier crop. Pick while young and stringless. Mildew resistant.

Oregon Sugarpod
A superb mangetout pea with flushes of broad, flat pods over an extended season. Must be picked while young and stringless and cooked whole.

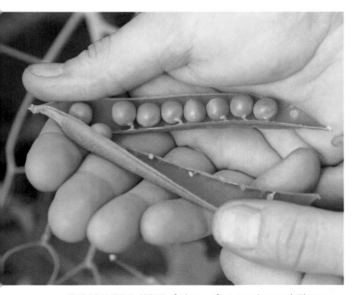

THE BEAUTIFUL SIGHT of nine perfect peas in a pod. These must be eaten fresh or cooked or frozen immediately if they are to be enjoyed at their best.

varieties, twiggy pea sticks, chicken wire attached to stakes or string and stakes are fine. For taller varieties, trellis, bamboo canes and netting are more appropriate. Blocks of semi-leafless peas are self-supporting. It is easy to underestimate just how sturdy such supports need to be, especially in windy weather. The foliage of fully grown plants acts like a sail, and everything could go flying, so make sure that the supports are strongly tethered. Once flowering has begun, plants must have enough water for the pods to swell properly. During dry spells check the soil moisture (dig under the surface near the plants to see if the soil is damp at root level) and if necessary give the crops a good soaking once or twice a week. Apply a thick organic mulch after watering to lock moisture in the ground.

At harvest time

Harvest peas regularly to ensure they are at the peak of freshness. Even if some pods are clearly past

MANY UNUSUAL VARIETIES of peas exist, such as this purple-podded example. They vary in yield and taste, and some are eaten pod and all while others are grown just for the seed.

exclude birds. To keep birds off, protect young plants with chicken wire, fleece or plastic netting. Once plants are growing strongly, bird attacks usually cease to be a problem.

Alternatively, start off plants under cover. Seed can be sown individually in root trainers or as groups in lengths of plastic guttering. First, cut the guttering to a convenient length and drill drainage holes in the bottom. Fill with a free-draining compost, water and allow to drain, then push in the seed 5cm (2in) apart.

When the plants are about 10cm (4in) high, gradually harden them off. Plant out by digging a gutter-shaped trench, and then simply slide the contents of the gutter pipe into it.

The tiny caterpillars of the pea moth can develop inside the pods, where they feed on the peas. Attacks can be very severe, in extreme cases they can wipe out entire crops. Pea moth usually spares very early and late crops. Protect mid-season crops with insect-proof mesh. Peas are also susceptible to powdery mildew in dry conditions in late summer. Grow resistant cultivars to avoid this problem.

their prime, take them off anyway to leave more resources for remaining pods. Pick from the bottom of the plant and work up. Eat or freeze as soon as possible after picking to retain the maximum flavour and nutrients.

After the harvest, do not pull up the spent crops, but cut off the stems at ground level. This is because the clusters of small white nodules found at the roots are full of nitrogen-fixing bacteria. If left in the ground these nodules will rot down, releasing their nitrogen back into the soil for the next crop to use.

Storing and cooking tips

The shoots and side shoots of pea plants taste remarkably like a fresh pea and make excellent additions to a salad. Use these shoots before the leaves have opened out.

Pests and diseases

Mice and birds devour seeds and seedlings. Catch mice, placing traps beneath upturned seed trays to

PEA MOTH can ruin crops and lead to disappointment as you pop open apparently healthy pods. Avoid the pest by growing early or late crops, or protecting with insect-proof mesh.

Perennial vegetables

Perennial vegetables, like herbaceous perennials, die down at the end of the year and re-sprout the following spring. They are are ideal for beginners, since they don't need specialist care and provide excellent value, cropping for many years. Some have extra benefits: globe and Jerusalem artichokes, for example, provide terrific architectural foliage and often have attractive flowers and seedheads; asparagus foliage can be used in cut-flower arrangements so these, and other larger vegetables such as rhubarb, can be grown in flower borders, freeing up valuable space in the vegetable garden.

Asparagus *Asparagus officinalis*

Asparagus spears are harvested each spring. Cutting then stops to allow the young shoots to develop foliage – essential for building up the plant's food reserves for future crops. It has a short harvest period of up to eight weeks, and it can be three years after first planting before the first crop. But it is worth it for a delicious crop that can last up to 20 years.

	J	F	M	A	M	J	J	A	S	O	N	D
Plant		▪	▪	▪								
Harvest				▪	▪							

The best sites and soils

Choose a sunny, sheltered site. Avoid frost pockets because they can damage emerging spears early in the season, and windy sites, which can snap off the mature fern, reducing the amount of food being stored in the crown. The fleshy crowns are likely to rot on waterlogged sites, so choose a well-drained soil and dig in plenty of organic matter before planting to improve soil structure.

Sowing and planting

It is much better to grow an all-male 'F1 hybrid' asparagus than an open-pollinated one, because the male plants are generally more productive. Female plants are less so because they produce seeds. There are two main ways to establish an asparagus bed, using either dormant crowns or seed. You can also buy pot-grown plants, but they are expensive. Crowns are more expensive than seed, but they can be cropped one year earlier.

Crowns Buy one-year-old crowns to plant in early spring, though some suppliers also send out crowns for autumn planting. It is important that the ground is ready on delivery because the fleshy crowns mustn't dry out. If planting is delayed, wrap up the roots in wet newspaper.

The bed system gives high yields in a relatively small space, with one bed consisting of three rows of crowns, spaced 30cm (12in) apart each way. On heavy soil, the bed can be slightly raised and mounded up to improve drainage. Then dig a trench for each row, 15cm (6in) deep, and carefully spread out the fragile crowns. Cover with 7.5cm (3in) of soil and water in well. Do not cut any emerging spears, and keep well watered during this first summer. Top up the trench to soil level in autumn.

Seed Sow in late winter. Soak the seed overnight, and then sow 1cm (½in) deep into 7.5cm (3in) pots of seed compost. Water well and keep at 14.5°C (58°F). Gradually harden off, acclimatizing the seedlings to life outdoors, and plant out at the same spacings for the crowns in early summer.

Cultivating the crop

Apply a balanced organic fertilizer and a 5cm (2in) thick mulch of organic matter in early spring before the spears emerge to help suppress weeds, retain moisture, protect the early spears from frost, and help prevent the soil forming a crust (called

TO PLANT one-year-old asparagus crowns, dig a trench for each row, 15cm (6in) deep, and carefully spread out the fragile crowns. Cover with 7.5cm (3in) of soil and water in well.

'capping') which causes bent spears. Top-dress with the same feed at the end of the harvest period.

As the foliage turns completely yellow in autumn, cut it down to the base. Remove any weeds as they appear. Use a hoe in autumn or early spring before the spears emerge. Hoeing is difficult because the plants are shallow-rooted, and the roots are easily damaged. Hand-weed those that appear during the growing season.

At harvest time

It is essential not to over-crop asparagus: if you do, future yields will be severely reduced. One-year old crowns of 'F1 hybrids' can be harvested for six weeks one year after planting (or two if they are open-pollinated), and for eight weeks in subsequent years. Seed-raised 'F1 hybrids' can be harvested for six weeks two years after planting (or three if open-pollinated), and for eight weeks thereafter.

Spears usually begin emerging around mid-spring. Cut off each spear just below soil level when it's roughly 20cm (8in) tall. It is essential to cut every spear, even those that are thin ('sprue') or bent ('crooks'), because this stimulates the dormant buds in the crown to grow.

Storing and cooking tips

Asparagus will keep for up to one week in the fridge, if stored upright in a small amount of water (replace the water daily). One of the best ways to cook asparagus is to boil in salted water for six or seven minutes, drain, and add butter, salt and ground black pepper. Steamers can be used to hold the spears

HARVEST ASPARAGUS SPEARS when they are about 20cm (8in) tall. Cut every spear, just below soil level, and this will ensure that dormant buds in the crown will begin to grow.

upright. Alternatively, brush with oil and fry on a griddle for six to eight minutes, turning frequently.

Pests and diseases

Occasionally slugs can nibble at emerging spears, but they don't pose a significant problem. The main pest is the asparagus beetle because both adults and larvae graze on the emerging spears and foliage. Adult beetles are 6mm (¼in) long, with black and white wing cases and a red under-body; larvae are dark grey, caterpillar-like and twice as long. Look for adults emerging in late spring, and pick off larvae and adults by hand. Burn the old foliage in the autumn in case any beetles are tucked in amongst it.

Recommended varieties

Cito
Popular with farmers as it is a dependable cropper under most conditions.

Gijnlim AGM
An early and consistently high yield of mid-green spears with purple tips.

Globe artichokes

" So many vegetables are such beautiful plants they are worth including in any garden for their looks. Two of the most statuesque perennial plants, the globe artichoke and the cardoon are also mouth-watering vegetables. They

are closely related – almost twins – and share the same stature and appearance. In spring their jagged grey leaves push through the middle of the desiccated clump of last year's plant. Within a matter of weeks they have put on good growth, and they continue to grow through summer making a magnificent show and providing real drama in the vegetable patch.

With cardoons, the base of the stem is eaten when young, but with artichokes it's the flowers or, more precisely, the calyx. The flower heads are severed before the flowers show and can be cooked in several ways. Each sepal, thick and fleshy, is dipped in butter and pulled off with your teeth or, when really young, the small heads can be stewed in olive oil and white wine.

Although artichokes are perennial, it is best to renew them every three years or they can become woody and unproductive. The best way to do this is by taking offsets from existing plants in March or April. Fresh, basal shoots on the outside of the plant are detached by sliding a sharp knife between the offset and the plant, and severing it below ground with roots already attached. They can be planted in fresh ground enriched with lots of muck. They always look a bit sad to begin with, but with a good watering they soon perk up.

Big plants, small eating; but the flavour justifies their space, and they are such magnificent plants, how could you not grow them? "

GLOBE ARTICHOKES are regal-looking plants, and every ornamental vegetable garden should have at least one.

Globe artichokes *Cynara scolymus*

The globe artichoke is highly ornamental and looks terrific in the flower border and vegetable garden. It is not known in the wild, and is derived from the cardoon, a native of the Mediterranean. It was imported into Europe by the Greeks and Romans. The edible part of the huge plants – the base of the mature flower bud – is small. Juvenile flower buds can also be eaten whole.

	J	F	M	A	M	J	J	A	S	O	N	D
Plant		■	■	■								
Harvest					■	■						

The best sites and soils

Globe artichokes aren't fully hardy and need a sunny, sheltered site with well-drained, moisture-retentive soil to which plenty of organic matter has been added. Avoid growing globe artichokes in shade or a frost pocket. Also avoid heavy soil that gets waterlogged in winter. The best yields are obtained in cool, moist summers that allow plants to build up plenty of foliage.

Sowing and planting

Buy globe artichokes as small, pot-grown plants, seeds or offsets. Grow plants 90cm (3ft) apart, or space them out in a big flower border, and remove any flower heads produced in the first year.

Potted plants are often sold as a 'globe artichoke' rather than a named variety, which implies that they have been grown from seed, in which case the quality will be variable. Named varieties are more reliable. Plant at any time, but ideally during spring or autumn.

Sow seed at 15°C (59°F) in late winter to early spring, sowing one seed per 9cm (3½in) pot filled with seed compost. Harden off seedlings gradually, and plant out in early summer. Since plants are very vulnerable to frost in their first winter, mulch them well and protect with a double-layered tent of horticultural fleece during frosts. Seed-raised plants are of variable quality, so remove weaker plants as they start to crop, and then propagate the best ones by offsets.

Cultivating the crop

Weed and water plants well in their first year. Though mature plants are drought-tolerant, better yields are obtained if they are watered during dry spells, especially during the period when flower buds are forming.

GLOBE ARTICHOKES should be grown in a sunny and sheltered site in well-drained, moisture-retaining soil.

Take rooted offsets (young plants attached to the parent) in early spring. Scrape the soil away from the parent, and remove the offset with a sharp knife, making sure you don't damage the roots. Trim back any over-long leaves and plant out the offset immediately, shading from any hot sun until it becomes established.

If one large flower head is required, remove the side shoots on each flower stem.

Regularly propagate offsets because globe artichokes crop best in their second and third years, after which they can be discarded. In autumn, cut off the old flower stems and tired foliage, and in spring mulch with well-rotted manure, keeping it away from the stems. Also apply a high potash liquid feed in spring and summer, alternatively add a general fertilizer in early spring. In exposed areas likely to experience prolonged frosts, mulch crowns with straw in late autumn, and remove it next spring.

At harvest time

Large terminal heads are produced in summer followed by a smaller, secondary flush. Harvest the artichokes with secateurs before the scales start to open or they will become tough. Since heat and drought can cause the heads to open rapidly, check plants regularly in such conditions. If you don't intend to eat the head straight away, leave a length of stalk attached and stand in a glass of water in the fridge, where it will keep for a week.

WHEN HARVESTING your artichokes, make sure that you cut the immature flower heads with secateurs just above a leaf junction.

Storing and cooking tips

Braise whole heads for 40 minutes in stock flavoured with wine, herbs, diced bacon, mushrooms and onion, and baste regularly. The tender sepals (like overlapping, fleshy leaves) of small heads, sepal bases of large heads, and the basal disk can be eaten in this way. Alternatively snap or cut off the sepals, remove the immature flower, and pare the base with a sharp knife to leave the artichoke heart. This can then also be braised. Plunge in water and lemon juice if not cooking immediately to avoid discolouration.

Recommended varieties

Green Globe
The standard green-headed variety with large, quality heads. If allowed to flower, it bears attractive, thistle-like blue flowerheads. They are best grown from offsets.

Purple Globe
A purple-headed globe artichoke with a fine flavour and attractive large, purple, thistle-like flowerheads. Grow from offsets.

Jerusalem artichokes

The one vegetable that always raises chuckles amongst those in the know is the Jerusalem artichoke. Eating them induces wind because the carbohydrates are not broken down by the intestines. Because of this the Jerusalem artichoke is not taken seriously, yet it is a delicious vegetable, extraordinarily productive even in poor soil, and it requires just the minimum amount of work. It stores well, providing valuable roots right through winter. Use it as the basis of warming soups, deep fry to make chips, and bake or combine it with sweet, dried fruits and spices in pies and other desserts.

In a good year its monumental stems – they can be up to 1.8-2.1m (6-7ft) high – are decked in yellow flowers. There's also lots of strong branching growth making an effective summer windbreak for an exposed site. When the foliage collapses after the frost, the knobbly tubers can be left in the ground and harvested as required. They are frost-hardy but shoveling a few centimetres of earth over the bed provides adequate insulation if conditions are severe. This is by far the best way of storing them. And any tubers left in the soil will grow again, so if the ground is needed for different crops, every trace of them must be removed.

All that is needed for a new planting is a few healthy tubers. They can be bought commercially but most people who are already growing Jerusalem artichokes will pass on a few. Although plants will grow well if muck or compost is added to the planting trench, it might well promote vegetative growth at the expense of tuber production. The flowers are insignificant so nipping out the growing tips, and therefore the flower buds, is sometimes recommended to help the plant concentrate its energies on tuber production – as if it needed any help!

BY LATE SUMMER, your Jerusalem artichokes will look like this (left), and small yellow sunflowers soon appear at the growing tips.

Jerusalem artichokes

Helianthus tuberosus

A member of the sunflower family, this artichoke comes from the cooler parts of North America. 'Jerusalem' is either a corruption of *girasole* (Italian for sunflower) or Ter Neuzen, the Dutch town that introduced it to England in 1617. The fleshy, knobbly tubers of this very hardy perennial contain the carbohydrate inulin as its storage material, rather than starch.

	J	F	M	A	M	J	J	A	S	O	N	D
Plant		■	■	■	■							
Harvest	■	■							■	■	■	

The best sites and soils

Ideally, provide a sunny position with well-drained, moisture-retentive soil. However, because the plant tolerates heavy, shady and dry sites, it can be raised in areas where other crops won't grow (such as under trees and next to hedges), although the yield will be lower. Artichokes also need careful positioning because of the shade they cast. The artichoke is a useful crop on new sites because its roots help break up the soil. It can also be grown as a windbreak since it grows to 3m (10ft) high when planted in two or three rows, but it will need support on open sites.

Sowing and planting

Tubers can be bought from the greengrocer, or named varieties of known quality can be bought from specialist suppliers. Larger tubers can be cut into egg-sized portions provided they have two or three buds. Enrich the site with organic matter and plant clean, healthy tubers in spring, each one 15cm (6in) deep and 60cm (24in) apart. If you are planting in rows, they'll need to be spaced 90cm (3ft) apart.

REMOVING AND SAVING THE TUBERS

If you don't want any Jerusalem artichokes next year, make sure that you dig them all – even the smallest – out of the ground or they'll regrow. Have a good root around, especially on sandy soil where they might be quite deep. If you are aiming to grow them again, save a few of the healthiest ones.

Cultivating the crop

Once stems are 30cm (12in) tall, pile up the earth around the roots to make plants more stable.

Recommended varieties

Fuseau
The long, relatively smooth tubers make this variety easy to prepare in the kitchen as they are easy to peel. The taste is said to be slightly smoky.

Stampede
An early-maturing variety with large tubers that have a very good texture and flavour.

ONCE THE PLANTS are mature in autumn, you can begin to dig out the tubers as and when you need them, as they don't store well out of the ground.

Weeding shouldn't be necessary because the quick-growing foliage smothers out other plants. There is also no need to feed.

You may need to stake plants on windy sites to deter wind-rock, which can cause the stems and the tubers to rot, reducing the yield. An alternative is to cut back any stems over 2m (6½ft) tall by about one-third, but don't be tempted to cut off any more, or the yield will suffer.

Plants initially produce foliage but, in midsummer, they bulk up their tubers, most of which have developed by mid-autumn. When the stems get frosted and die back in late autumn, cut back the plants to 15cm (6in) above the soil.

The tubers will survive perfectly well in the ground, but over winter it is best to provide a mulch of old stems, straw or newspaper to protect them.

WHEN HARVESTING the plants, you can pull them out in whole clumps at a time. Each plant will provide about a dozen tubers.

At harvest time

Harvest tubers as and when they are needed, but they do store fairly well out of the ground with their thick skins. The flavour is said to improve after a frost. Expect at least a dozen tubers from each plant.

Storage and cooking tips

Store tubers in the ground or, if it is likely to be frozen solid, waterlogged or colonized by slugs and snails, store them in moist sand in a cool, frost-free place such as a shed. Jerusalem artichokes can also be stored in a perforated plastic bag in the fridge for a couple of weeks. The tubers can be scrubbed and roasted, or sliced thinly and fried like crisps. Once peeled, they can be made into soup or mixed with butter, seasoned and mashed. Peeled and thickly sliced, they make an excellent gratin.

Pests and diseases

Slugs and snails can hollow out tubers and like to eat the young shoots. Biological controls can be used provided the ground is kept moist, and the soil temperature is over 4.5°C (40°F).

Root aphids can feed on the roots and reduce plant vigour. Signs of attack are plants wilting in the sun and weak growth. On lifting the plants, their roots will be colonized by yellow-brown aphids which excrete a white, waxy powder. No control is available, but watering and feeding the plants to improve their health may help them survive an attack. If the attack is sustained, the best solution is often to plant new tubers on a fresh site.

Rhubarb

Rheum x cultorum

Although the edible stems of rhubarb are treated like a fruit in sweet puddings, it is truly a vegetable. Related species can be found in the ornamental garden, but this is a plant best confined to the vegetable plot. The plants can be forced to produce an early crop with longer stems; placing terracotta forcing jars over the crowns is the traditional method.

	J	F	M	A	M	J	J	A	S	O	N	D
Plant	■	■	■	■						■	■	■
Harvest				■	■	■						

The best sites and soils

Provide a sunny position and well-drained, moisture-retentive, fertile soil. Before establishing a new bed, add plenty of organic matter and remove all perennial weeds. Rhubarb needs a cold period to break winter dormancy before spring growth starts, but it shouldn't be sited in a frost pocket. Also avoid heavy soil which can rot the fleshy crowns. Cool, moist summers and dry winters provide optimum growing conditions.

Sowing and planting

Rhubarb can be bought as dormant crowns, pot-grown plants or seed. One or two plants should be enough for most people, but if more are required, space plants 1m (3½ft) apart. Whichever method you choose, don't harvest until the second year.

Dormant crowns Buy crowns from reputable suppliers, who sell reliable stock. Plant in late autumn with the dormant buds just above the soil, and keep well watered for the first growing season.

GROW RHUBARB in a sunny position and in well-drained, moisture-retentive, fertile soil that has been prepared with lots of organic matter.

CREATING VIGOROUS NEW PLANTS

Plants should be divided every three to four years otherwise they can become congested and weak. Mark healthy plants in the spring, and in late autumn dig up the base to expose the rhizome (like an underground piece of ginger). Divide it into good-sized sections with a spade, ensuring that each has at least two healthy, undamaged buds. Replant the divisions immediately. If dividing large clumps, discard the older, less productive centre portion.

Pot-Grown plants They can be more expensive than crowns, but can be planted at any time of year, ideally in spring or autumn. There's a more limited choice of varieties than with crowns.

Seed The cheapest method. Plants are generally virus-free, but they can be variable in quality. Sow in early or mid-spring in a prepared seedbed, or in 9cm (3½in) pots, then select the most vigorous seedlings. Harden off and plant out in early or mid-summer, harvesting for only four weeks in their second year.

Cultivating the crop

Rhubarb responds well to feeding, especially with nitrogen. A spring top-dressing of pelleted poultry manure or well-rotted farmyard manure helps. Don't apply directly onto the crown: that encourages rotting. Water plants well in their first season.

Forcing A technique for obtaining earlier, more tender stems. Early-cropping varieties are most suitable; crops can be forced in the ground or lifted. For forcing in the ground, cover healthy crowns

RHUBARB FORCERS are specially designed pots used to encourage the growth of early, tender stems. Check that the plants are slug- and snail-free and cover them in early January.

TO PULL RHUBARB, grab the stem at its base, close to the crown of the plant, and pull it down with a slight twist. Stems come away easily.

with a rhubarb forcer or large, tall pot in mid-winter. Forcing can be hastened by mounding farmyard manure or garden compost around the forcer to heat it. Once shoots appear, check them daily and harvest in two to four weeks. Do not force the same crowns year after year.

To force by lifting, dig up healthy crowns and leave them exposed for 7–10 days. Move them into a shed, cellar or garage with a constant temperature of between 15–17°C (59–62°F): any warmer and they'll rot. Put them in pots of compost and keep just moist. Exclude all light, but ventilate at night to deter rotting. Harvest in late winter.

At harvest time

Stems can be harvested until midsummer, after which they become rather tough and green. Stopping then also allows the plant to produce sufficient foliage to build up food reserves for next year. Remove no more than half the stalks at one time, harvesting as soon as the leaves open fully. To remove a stalk, hold it at the base, pull down and twist.

Storing and cooking tips

Store washed and dried stems in a clear plastic bag in the fridge for two weeks. Rhubarb also freezes well, and there is no need to blanch it first. Rhubarb stems can be stewed in a little water and sugar for crumbles, tarts and pies; it is also used to make preserves and a medium-sweet wine.

Pests and diseases

Slugs and snails will eat young shoots, especially those being forced. Crowns can be infected with honey fungus, in which case dispose of affected and surrounding plants – but do not compost them. If plants are weak or the foliage is mottled or distorted, dig them up and discard them. Replace with healthy, virus-free stock obtained from a reputable supplier.

Recommended varieties

Timperley Early AGM
A consistently good variety that crops early with thick, high-yielding stems. Performs well outside but was bred for forcing, which improves the colour.

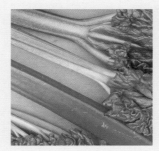

Victoria
Easily raised from seed to produce delicious, juicy, medium-sized stems. It forces well.

Root and stem vegetables

You must make room for at least a few of these wonderfully productive crops. Although their bounty is mostly hidden from view, either buried in the ground or hidden below foliage, this secret harvest includes valued vegetables, such as potatoes, carrots and beetroots. Not only will root and stem crops be able to sustain you through the winter months, since they store well, they will also be delicious on your summer plate, from shredded beetroot or carrot on salads, delicious new potatoes in the spring, and fennel bulbs roasted with olive oil, Parmesan and balsamic vinegar.

Beetroots

" Lots of vegetables get a bad press, and beetroot gets one of the worst. Perhaps school dinners put us off, or more likely beetroot pickled in strong malt vinegar ruining its taste. But the tide is changing, and the humble beet is being increasingly valued as a tasty and unique ingredient in salads, soups and stews. When young and tender it is delicious raw. And it's not just the roots that are mouth-watering. Its pretty foliage makes a fine addition to a salad bowl: the bright green, purple-veined leaves glistening with a dressing add colour and taste to any green salad. In fact when it was first grown, it was valued mainly for its leaves, its roots being used medicinally to treat a large number of ailments from fevers to skin problems, and it was not until the Middle Ages that beetroot was regularly grown for its roots. This seems strange since beetroot keeps so well. In sand or soil it stays in good shape right through winter, and it can be harvested even in cold weather.

Personally, I prefer my beetroot small and, when space is limited, it's a lovely idea to squeeze little rows of beetroot in here and there, sowing them successionally, perhaps every fortnight. Beetroot takes from eight to ten weeks to mature. First sowings can be made under cloches, but there is a greater chance of these plants running to seed and throwing up flowering stems which make the roots woody and hard, and quite inedible. You can choose bolt-resistant varieties, but it is probably better to wait until the soil has warmed up a bit. The plants will soon catch up. Alternatively, sow the seed individually in cells or modules and give it some protection, planting out the young seedlings promptly because they mustn't have their growth checked or they may fail to make the plump roots you need. Each seed is actually a fruit composed of three or four seeds. If they all germinate you will need to thin them out carefully leaving just one seedling per station, otherwise you will have to wait longer for them to reach eating size.

Even young beets take quite a time to cook. To maintain their earthy flavour try baking them (the skins squeeze off easily) or just eat them whole, skin and all. Their taste, in a dish with young broad beans, is heavenly. One mouthful and you'll vow to carry on growing your own vegetables forever. "

YOU CAN GROW a mature crop of beetroot in less than 10 weeks, making it ideal for squeezing in between other crops.

Beetroots *Beta vulgaris*

Forms of the common beetroot are grown for their high sugar content (sugar beet), as animal feed (mangel wurzels), for their edible leaves, which also look good as border edging, and most commonly for their roots, which are usually blood red. They are tasty when fresh, grated or sliced, cooked or raw – with just a dash of orange or lemon juice.

	J	F	M	A	M	J	J	A	S	O	N	D
Sow		■	■	■	■	■	■	■				
Harvest							■	■	■	■	■	

The best sites and soils

Grow in an open, sunny site in well-drained, fertile soil. The best crops grow in soil that has been improved with well-rotted organic matter previously. About one week before sowing, apply a balanced general fertilizer. Light, free-draining soil produces the best early crops because it warms up more quickly than heavier ground, although heavy soils can be pre-warmed by putting cloches in place for several weeks before sowing.

Sowing and planting

Most beetroot varieties produce rounded or globe-shaped roots, while there are also long and cylindrical

THINNING

Seedlings should be thinned as soon as their first true leaves appear because a delay can result in small or distorted roots. Under cloches, thin to leave the strongest seedling in each group. In rows, thin to leave 10cm (4in) between seedlings if you want large beetroot, or grow at 5cm (2in) spacings for baby beets. The exception is monogerm varieties which produce only one strong seedling per cluster.

or stump-rooted types that are best for winter storage. As with all vegetables, 'F1 hybrids' produce the most uniform crop.

The large, corky-textured seed is easy to handle but can be slow to germinate. The first sowing should be in late winter or early spring under cloches, horticultural fleece or frames, or in the open if you live in a very mild area, because beetroot doesn't germinate well below 7.5°C (45°F). Space beetroot seeds with about a thumb width between them.

Sow outdoors from early spring to summer. In order to have a regular supply of tender roots, sow a short row every couple of weeks. Mark out straight rows using a string line or bamboo cane, water the drill if the soil is dry, and sow the seed thinly, 2.5cm (1in) deep, in rows 30cm (12in) apart. Seedlings should appear in 10–14 days. Thin to 10cm (4in) between seedlings as soon as possible.

In mild areas, you can try your luck by sowing an overwintered crop in mid- to late summer to mature

THE BEST WAY to make beetroot seed germinate is to soak it overnight. Sow extra short rows every 14 days to provide a continuous crop.

the following spring; the foliage of some varieties becomes a beautiful dark red in cold weather.

Cultivating the crop

Beetroot is a trouble-free crop, but as a rough guide, water thoroughly every 10–14 days during dry spells. Lack of water causes woody roots; a fluctuation in water supply can cause splitting; and an excess means leaves at the expense of roots. Regularly hand-weed close to the plants and hoe the soil between the rows, but keep the blade well away from the roots because they will 'bleed' if damaged.

At harvest time

For the best flavour and texture, harvest when the roots reach tennis-ball size: any larger and they develop an unpleasant, woody texture. Succulent and tender baby beets can be harvested as soon as they're large enough to eat, usually around golf-ball size. Before lifting, use a garden fork to loosen the soil beneath, but take care not to damage the roots, particularly if they're intended for storage.

Storing and cooking tips

Beetroot stores well and will keep through winter. Lift the roots in early or mid-autumn, and select only sound ones for storage. Gently knock off any surplus soil and twist off the leaves several centimetres from the top of the root, wearing rubber gloves to avoid staining your hands. Then carefully place the roots, not touching each other, in boxes of dry sand or coir. Store in a cool shed or garage. Small, succulent beet is delicious eaten raw, but boil larger ones until tender.

THE EASIEST WAY to harvest a crop of beetroot is to ease a fork or trowel under the soil, enabling you to lift the swollen roots gently out of the ground.

Recommended varieties

Pablo
A very early variety with smooth skin, fine colour and free from internal rings. It has good resistance to bolting.

Boltardy
Recommended for early sowing, this is a smooth skinned, bolt-resistant variety with a fine colour.

Carrots

"Crunchy carrots come close to the top of my list of favourite vegetables. For a start they are so versatile – pull them young, wash them, and eat raw. The taste is poles apart from that of the 'manufactured' carrots of supermarket shelves. Home-grown organic baby carrots are a delicacy, but pull them in the middle of winter when something earthy and comforting is required and the same roots, grown to maturity, are instantly warming and filling.

Given how much I love them, it's ironic that they are so difficult to grow at Glebe Cottage. Carrots love sandy soil and their ancestor, the wild carrot, loves a seaside home where it flourishes in light, well-drained soil. On my heavy clay the roots struggle to push themselves down into the soil and expand into anything approaching a respectable root. The other problem is that even if the soil has been lightened using compost and sand, the roots are almost invariably attacked by carrot root fly. The larvae of this horrible pest burrow into the surface of the carrot, sometimes right into its centre. From above there is no sign of the damage that lies underneath the soil. The carrot fly is devious, it flies just above ground level, completely invisible, and when it picks up the aroma of carrot in it goes, laying its eggs close to the infant root. Since

TO MATCH THIS healthy, prolific crop, you'll need protection against carrot root fly and, ideally, light, free-draining soil.

we don't use chemicals here (if they kill the larvae they will hardly do us any good), we either stop growing them at all or put up a fly barrier. The best is a fine mesh specifically designed for the job.

One way to combat poor soil is to grow carrots in containers, sowing them successionally so that each pot reaches maturity at a different time, one after the other. A fortnight between sowings from early spring right through until autumn provides a constant supply. Wherever you sow your carrots, sow them sparingly, and thin them on a cool, rainy day because the carrot fly can identify its target with ease in hot, sunny weather. Next year I'm going to try growing maincrop carrots in open ground with mesh around them, and large pots with a sprinkle of seed for baby carrots through the season.

Although they are thought of as savoury, carrots bridge the gap between sweet and savoury. In India there are several sweets whose basic ingredient is the carrot. Try cooking your carrots with a little butter and a splash of marsala and a drop of water. Keep the lid on the pan and shake fairly often. The melting flesh of the carrots is imbued with all the taste of the wine and get glazed to a delicious amber colour."

Carrots *Daucus carota*

Choose the right varieties and you can harvest carrots from mid-May to March. They store well over winter and come in a range of shapes and colours – from red to yellow to purple. You may find it difficult to grow the perfectly shaped carrot, but by way of compensation you are more likely to grow something with excellent flavour and texture.

	J	F	M	A	M	J	J	A	S	O	N	D
Sow	▪	▪	▪	▪	▪	▪	▪					
Harvest	▪	▪	▪		▪	▪	▪	▪	▪	▪	▪	▪

The best sites and soils

All carrots require an open, sunny site and well-drained fertile soil, but you need to find out exactly what type of soil you've got and choose varieties to suit. To grow long-rooted carrots you need a good loam (see page 22) or sandy soil that can be deeply cultivated to at least one spade's depth. If your soil is shallow, stony or heavy clay, then opt for stump-rooted or round carrots rather than long-rooted types which are likely to develop stunted or forked roots. If the soil is completely unsuitable or space is limited, try short-rooted types in containers or growbags.

Sowing and planting

Sow the first crop in late winter or early spring under cloches or frames, or outdoors if you live in a mild area, to harvest around late spring. Outdoors, sow from early spring. Seeds will germinate more quickly if the soil is warm, having been covered with polythene for several weeks.

MANURING CARROT BEDS

Carrots produce the best crops in ground that has been improved by incorporating plenty of organic matter. Although there is no evidence that organic matter causes roots to fork, it is traditional to omit carrots for a year after manuring.

Choose a variety to suit the sowing time. Early varieties should be sown about mid-spring, then switch to maincrop varieties for the rest of spring and summer. For a regular supply, sow every three to four weeks until late summer.

Deeply dig the ground in winter and then rake to a fine tilth in spring as soon as soil conditions permit. If the soil sticks to your boots, it's too wet for raking. About a week before sowing, apply a balanced general fertilizer and rake into the soil.

Use a string line or bamboo cane to mark out lines, then make shallow drills using a draw hoe or trowel to create drills 1cm (½in) deep with 15cm (6in) between the rows. If the soil is dry, water the drill and allow it to drain before sowing. Sprinkle the fine seed along the drill, cover with a thin layer of soil and firm down.

Sow carrots sparingly to avoid the need for thinning later on because the scent of the crushed foliage attracts the carrot root fly. Growing carrots with other plants like spring onions or annual flowers (such as cornflowers and larkspurs) is a traditional but not very effective way of limiting carrot fly damage. Carrots still produce a good crop even when grown cheek-by-jowl with these other plants.

Cultivating the crop

Carrots are a drought resistant crop and relish hot weather, seldom needing water. If they wilt and go grey, however, a thorough soak every 10–14 days will help. Weed every couple of weeks by hoeing between the rows, and hand-weed close to the plants to avoid damaging the roots. Thin to around 5cm (2in) between plants, using the thinnings as baby carrots as soon as possible. Thinning or weeding is best done in the evening to reduce the smell from the foliage, and easier if you water the crop several hours beforehand.

From late spring to summer, cover or surround the crop with a barrier of fleece, fine mesh or polythene to prevent an attack of carrot fly. The low-flying insects lay their eggs next to the plants, and the larvae then tunnel into and eat the carrots, leaving unsightly holes.

At harvest time

Carrots are ready for harvesting about 12–16 weeks after sowing, although the timing depends on whether you prefer tender baby carrots or larger roots. Young carrots can be pulled up carefully by hand, while larger ones and those intended for storage are best lifted by gently easing them up with a fork to avoid damaging or breaking the roots.

Storing and cooking tips

Carrots keep best in the soil. Remove the foliage in late autumn and cover with 15cm (6in) of straw or a thick layer of cardboard. Keep out rain with some

SURROUND CARROTS with a 50cm (20in) barrier to exclude the carrot fly, which flies close the ground.

polythene. Where soils become waterlogged in winter, carrots can be lifted and stored in boxes of sand, but their flavour and texture suffers as a result.

The sweet flavour and vitamin content are highest in roots that are scrubbed and eaten raw. If you prefer carrots cooked, however, then steaming them gives the best results.

Recommended varieties

Adelaide AGM
Excellent early crop, suitable for sowing in frames. This variety forms stump-ended roots, is almost coreless and has fine tops.

Parmex AGM
A round-rooted carrot, ideal for shallow soils and growing in containers. It has good uniformity and core colour.

Flyaway
A maincrop variety, of medium length, with stump-ended roots and sweet orange flesh. This carrot has good natural resistance to carrot fly.

Maestro AGM
A blunt, smooth-skinned carrot, uniform in shape and size. This variety is popular with organic gardeners.

Celeriac *Apium graveolens*

Celeriac is much easier to grow than celery, and easily slots into spare gaps in the garden, forming neat clumps of celery-like leaves. Beneath its slightly odd, gnarled appearance lies delicious creamy, potato-like flesh with a subtle, celery-like flavour. The similarity to celery stops at the taste, because celeriac is a far less time-consuming crop to grow.

	J	F	M	A	M	J	J	A	S	O	N	D
Sow			■	■								
Plant				■	■	■						
Harvest	■	■	■	■					■	■	■	■

The best sites and soils

Choose ground in full sun or partial shade. In the wild, celeriac grows in moist soils, but well-drained, moisture-retentive soil is ideal. In autumn, improve the soil's water-holding capacity by digging in generous amounts of organic matter (e.g. garden compost or well-rotted manure).

Sowing and planting

Sow the tiny seed in early spring to give the crop plenty of time to grow to a good size. Sow thinly in pots or modules filled with seed compost mixed in equal parts with fine vermiculite. Then cover the seed with vermiculite, and germinate in a propagator at a temperature of about 15°C (59°F). Transfer the pot-grown seedlings into individual biodegradable pots of multipurpose compost once the first true leaves have formed, with one plant per section. Make sure the plants have good light and that the temperature stays above 10°C (50°F). The seedlings should be acclimatized to outdoor conditions before being planted out at the end of spring or early summer. Space the seedlings 30cm (12in) apart in rows 45cm (18in) apart, and water in. Protect the young seedlings from slugs and snails.

Cultivating the crop

Water plants every 5–10 days if no rain falls. In midsummer, cut off the lower leaves to expose more of the crown. Also remove any blistered leaves, which may be sign of attack by the celery leaf miner larvae. In early autumn, draw soil around the swollen stem-bases to keep the flesh white. Protect the plants in the ground over winter during really cold spells with a covering of straw.

At harvest time

Harvest from mid-autumn to early spring when the celeriac is between the size of an apple and a

A WELL-GROWN, well-tended celeriac is quite a sight, and can easily rival a coconut in size. Make sure that seedlings have enough room to expand.

THOROUGHLY WATER emerging celeriac every 5–10 days during dry spells, adding a high-nitrogen fertilizer if growth is poor.

ALLOW SIX MONTHS for celeriac to mature. Ease the roots out of the ground with a fork and trim off foliage and fine roots.

coconut. On light soil, celeriac can remain in the ground all winter and be harvested when required. On heavier ground, and soil prone to waterlogging, harvest in late autumn and store.

Storing and cooking tips

To store celeriac, twist off the leafy tops and place the vegetable in boxes of damp peat or coir in a cool shed. It can also be diced and lightly blanched for storage in the freezer. Celeriac is a hugely versatile vegetable and can be used in soups and salads. The French grate it into a Dijon mustard mayonnaise to create coleslaw-like *rémoulade*. It can also be fried, roasted and mashed with potato.

Recommended varieties

Monarch AGM
A smooth-skinned variety with tender flesh which can be harvested from early autumn.

Brilliant
This variety has large, round fleshy roots of good quality and an excellent taste. It stores well after harvesting.

Florence fennel

" There are some vegetables that combine handsome good looks, marvellous texture and delectable taste in one package and, for me, Florence fennel or finnochio is a prime example. There are two main types, one that forms fairly flat bulbs and one that makes spheres of white flesh. The latter is more tender; the former has a more concentrated aniseed flavour.

I had never managed to grow Florence fennel well here. Because it's a Mediterranean crop, I tried sowing it early, on the premise that it must need a long season, but each time I tried, it bolted, producing flowers without forming the great white, crunchy-leaf bases that I craved.

The problem is that if it experiences periods of cold temperatures after it has started to grow, it attempts to flower and set seed. The trick is to sow or plant it out after the threat of plummeting temperatures has passed, say in late spring or early summer.

Being a fast-growing plant there should be plenty of time for it to develop its big white swollen stems, unchecked by fluctuating temperatures. In California, where it was probably introduced by the Spanish centuries ago, it has made itself at home both in cultivation and in the kitchen. The Mediterranean-type climate means it can be sown in late winter and early spring and can be harvested about ten weeks later.

Florence fennel hates root disturbance. It is a member of the Umbel family and, without exception, they all resent being transplanted. There is no reason, however, not to plant one or two seeds per module, taking out the weakest if both germinate, and setting out the young plant when it is fairly sturdy. This is a good way of stealing a march on the season: plants suffer no check to their growth since their roots remain intact.

Sowing successively isn't realistic, but Florence fennel can be harvested for several weeks, if not months, from the same sowing, and it will provide anything from a slender adolescent to a full-blown, mature vegetable. "

THREE MONTHS FROM SEED to the table, fennel makes a swollen, crunchy, white, aniseed-tasting bulb. Water well, not letting the soil bake dry in summer.

Florence fennel *Foeniculum vulgare*

Well-known as a garden herb, the swollen edible bulb of the fennel plant – known as Florence fennel – is a popular vegetable in Italy, from where it was introduced to northern Europe. Unfortunately, it has a habit of flowering rapidly if conditions aren't quite as Mediterranean as it would like, and if this happens the bulb will not swell. The fine, feathery foliage is very decorative.

	J	F	M	A	M	J	J	A	S	O	N	D
Sow				▪	▪	▪	▪					
Plant					▪	▪	▪					
Harvest					▪	▪	▪	▪				

The best sites and soils

Florence fennel is fussy. It thrives in a sunny, sheltered site with rich, moisture-retentive soil, ideally free-draining and with lots of organic matter. Avoid heavy clay, stony, or poorly drained ground. Probably best not to bother growing it if you can't meet its exacting requirements, because the plants will bolt if they become stressed.

Sowing and planting

Since Florence fennel is frost-tender, seed can either be started under cover for an earlier crop, or sown in open ground for a later harvest once danger of frost is past. The plants should mature around 14–16 weeks after sowing.

When raising plants under cover, it's important to keep root disturbance to a minimum and avoid bolting. Seed should therefore be sown in pots or modular trays to allow transplanting with the minimum of stress from mid- to late spring. Fill containers with seed compost, firm gently, water

HERB AND VEGETABLE FENNEL are both prolific flowerers, attracting bees. Save the seed for sowing next years' crop under cover, or after the last frost.

FEATHERY SHOOTS

When harvesting, cut the bulb off just above ground level and leave the stump in the ground. Young feathery shoots will soon appear, and they can be used in the kitchen.

well and allow to drain. In each pot, sow several seeds 1cm (½in) deep, spaced a little apart from each other, then cover with compost. Place in a greenhouse or on a sunny windowsill and, once the seed has germinated, thin to leave one seedling per pot. Keep plants evenly moist, and plant out in around four to five weeks, but don't leave them in their pots for too long or they're likely to bolt.

When sowing seed in the garden from late spring to mid-summer, mark out straight lines and make a shallow drill 1cm (½in) deep. Water if dry, and allow to drain before sowing the seed thinly. Space rows 45cm (18in) apart. It's a good idea to make several sowings over a period of several weeks as insurance against poor germination or bolting caused by low or fluctuating temperatures.

Cultivating the crop

Container-grown plants can be planted out from late spring to very early summer, depending on whether you live in a mild or cold area. Acclimatize plants to outdoor conditions for a couple of weeks, then plant out at 20cm (8in) spacings and water in well. The direct-sown seedlings need to be thinned once they have germinated and are growing strongly, leaving around 20cm (8in) between each plant.

Keep well watered during dry spells. Weed the crop regularly, hoeing between the rows and hand-weeding close to the plants. As the bulbs start to swell, use a hoe or trowel to pile up the soil around the roots to make them whiter and sweeter.

At harvest time

Harvest from late summer to mid-autumn once the bulbs are sufficiently large, using a fork to loosen the roots carefully before lifting.

When harvesting, cut the bulb off just above ground level and leave the stump in the ground. Young feathery shoots will soon appear, and these can also be used in the kitchen.

FLATTISH BULBS are nearly as rewarding as rounded ones and can be harvested for the table as soon as they are ready. The foliage can be used as a herb dressing.

Storing and cooking tips

The succulent, aniseed-flavoured stems are rich in potassium and folic acid while the attractive, feathery foliage can be used in the same way as the herb, although the flavour is stronger. Florence fennel is superb with fish and in casseroles. The raw root can also be grated or shredded for salads. The bulb will keep for several weeks if stored in a cool, dry place.

Recommended varieties

Sirio
A quick maturing variety, which can be sown in July for autumn harvesting. It has large bulbs with a sweet flavour.

Victorio AGM
This variety produces round, smooth, pure white bulbs with neat feathery foliage and good resistance to bolting.

Parsnips

The sweet, nutty taste of baked parsnips epitomizes being indoors on a cold winter's day – the sugar in the parsnip lightly caramelized and sticky, the skin glistening, the interior creamy and squashy. We don't eat meat in our house, but we still have a typical Christmas dinner with roast vegetables, bread sauce, stuffing and gravy. The roast potatoes are important, but what makes it are the parsnips baked in olive oil.

My soil is not ideal for parsnips, being too heavy and cold, and sometimes wet. Prize-winning parsnips need deep, sandy soil that is also fertile. I should probably try one of the modern short-rooted varieties that are ideal for small gardens and containers: a few big pots of parsnips will produce a decent yield and are relatively trouble-free. Parsnips do take a long time to grow and mature, but on the other hand they need little attention and they can be left in the ground after the frosts have

PARSNIPS CAN BE LIFTED in late summer or after the first frosts.

started. In fact freezing actually improves their flavour and, though you can take them out of the ground and store them in sand or boxes, they may as well stay where they are, growing until they are needed.

Parsnips are closely related to carrots and, like the rest of their kin, are slow to germinate. The wild parsnip actually produces a number of fake seeds, with no embryo, around the edge of the flat head of small, yellow flowers. This is an insurance policy. Insects and animals might nibble around the edge, but the fertile seeds have a good chance of being left intact. Cultivated parsnip seeds, however, tend not to display this characteristic and germination is highly reliable.

Sow parsnip seed only in warm conditions. It's unlikely to germinate in the cold, so delay your sowings until at least mid-spring; early sowings are also more prone to parsnip canker. Many gardeners often sow something with the parsnip to germinate quickly so that the row (or patch) is marked as soon as possible. Radishes are a good choice because they germinate rapidly, and can be harvested while the young parsnip seedlings are growing. Another idea, especially suitable when sowing parsnips in a block, is to mix the seed with hardy annuals – you could use a cornfield mix of poppies, corn cockle and corn marigolds. Sow the mix sparingly, and thin when the plants are several centimetres high, making sure you leave the parsnips in the ground.

Our modern parsnip has been developed from the wild parsnip, a delightful meadow plant that can grow up to 1.5–1.8m (5–6ft) high, branching as it goes and producing an array of lime-green yellow flowers. The Greeks and Romans valued it, and the Emperor Tiberius imported parsnips from the Rhine Valley. It's most often grown in Northern Europe where it develops its full taste as the starches turn to sugar in the cold.

Parsnips *Pastinaca sativa*

Parsnips are biennial, completing their life-cycle of flowering and setting seed over two years. They are extremely hardy, and can be left in the ground over winter and harvested when needed. It is well worth leaving a few roots unharvested to develop their pretty spring flowers, which attract many beneficial predatory insects, including hoverflies, to the garden.

	J	F	M	A	M	J	J	A	S	O	N	D
Sow		■	■	■	■							
Harvest	■	■	■						■	■	■	■

The best sites and soils

Although it takes time and skill to grow the perfectly tapered, prize-winning roots that are the stars of the village show, growing some for the dinner table requires no special skill. Parsnips like a sunny position and grow well in most well-drained soils, ideally one that is light and sandy. Choose a site that was improved with well-rotted compost or manure the previous year, and about a week before sowing, rake the soil over thoroughly, adding a general fertilizer,

THE KEY to getting a good crop is to select the strongest seedling from each sowing, and to make sure that the crops are well spaced and the rows are well weeded.

then rake the surface to a fine, crumbly texture to prepare a seedbed. Forking of roots is a common problem with parsnips; do not add organic matter to the soil the same season as sowing, and if the soil is shallow, or heavy and stony, then choose a bulbous variety.

Sowing and planting

The seed of parsnips is notoriously slow to germinate, taking a few weeks before the first signs appear. For this reason, it is possible to sow fast-maturing vegetables, such as radishes, around them so that you are able to make good use of the available space.

Always sow resistant varieties to avoid canker, which results in rough, reddish brown areas around the top of the root. Parsnip seed stores badly, so always use a fresh batch each year. The seed can be sown from late winter, but results are often more satisfactory if you wait a couple of months, especially in colder areas or on heavy clay soils. Later sowings can also be less prone to canker.

Make a drill 1cm (½in) deep in the prepared seedbed with a hoe. If the bottom of the drill is dry, dampen it first. Sow three seeds every 15cm (6in), and then lightly cover them with fine soil.

The rows should be spaced approximately 30cm (12in) apart.

Cultivating the crop

When the seedlings appear, thin out to leave the strongest one of the three, and hoe regularly to keep competing weeds down. Large easy-to-peel roots are obtained by wide spacing of plants and the absence of weeds. Parsnips are highly drought-resistant plants that only need watering once every 10–14 days if the foliage begins to wilt.

At harvest time

Start lifting parsnips in late summer as baby vegetables, digging them up carefully with a fork. Most gardeners wait until the foliage has died back and the first frosts have arrived, however, which is a sign that the roots have begun to sweeten. A hard frost will turn the starch content of parsnips into sugars, which is why parsnips make a popular winter vegetable, and they are at their sweetest during the coldest winters. Parsnips can be left in the ground until they are needed, but during hard frosts it may be impossible to dig them out of the soil.

Pests and diseases

Like carrots, parsnips suffer from carrot root fly (see pages 134-135). If the crop is peppered with tiny holes on harvest, cover or surround future crops with low fences of horticultural fleece, fine mesh or polythene from late spring to early autumn to stop the fly laying its eggs. Cut off any leaves with brown, dried-up patches as they may be caused by the celery leaf miner pest, which is the larvae of a small fly.

Storing and cooking tips

The virtues of parsnips have been appreciated by generations of gardeners for over 2,000 years. Although parsnips are winter hardy, you can lift some for storage in late autumn so that you've always got some in case the ground is too hard to dig. Arrange the roots in boxes so that they are not touching, in layers of sand or peat, and place in a dry shed. Cut the roots into 'fingers', removing any central woody parts, and roast or fry with garlic to bring out the rich, sweet flavour and unusual fibrous texture. Parsnips can also be thinly sliced and fried to make chips or crisps.

Recommended varieties

Javelin AGM
A wedge shaped, canker-resistant parsnip with a good yield. This variety has long slender roots and a good flavour.

Gladiator AGM
Good for a light sandy soil, this variety is early to mature, canker-resistant and has large, smooth white roots with a sweet flavour. Good for any soil.

Countess AGM
A reliable, smooth-skinned, canker-resistant parsnip with a lovely sweet, pale cream flesh. The yields are very good.

Excalibur AGM
A long, cream-coloured parsnip, suitable for harvest from September onwards. The white skinned roots have a sweet flavour and are canker-resistant.

Potatoes

" Is it worth growing your own potatoes? They are the most readily available of all vegetables. You can pick up a bag of 'Red Duke of York' from the garage on your way home or buy a few kilos of 'Ratte' when you're doing your weekly shop. But one very good reason for growing spuds in the garden is that you can grow the type you like. You can choose exactly the variety you want for its flavour or specific culinary use, and harvest it when you need it or store it over winter.

It is true that potatoes take up lots of room, but can you grow a few plants on even the smallest balcony or in a tiny backyard in pots or containers? The flavour of home-grown potatoes is so concentrated, so earthy, it is almost like eating another vegetable, definitely different from the bland, well-washed supermarket specials.

Most of us regard our spuds as precisely that – ours. If you are Irish, so are your spuds; the Welsh eat Welsh potatoes, the Scots Scottish potatoes, and every self-respecting Englishman knows that potatoes are English. But we are all wrong. The potato is

MAINCROP POTATOES are ready to harvest after the foliage has died back.

South American, but since its introduction in the 15th century it has changed our dietary habits. It isn't hardy, but, since it grows rapidly, there is plenty of time for its tubers to swell under the soil and for us to harvest it before the winter frosts.

Digging potatoes is everyone's favourite job. Not a chore but a real pleasure. Once you start uncovering the hidden treasure you want to dig endlessly. The number of tubers you uncover is a revelation. This is one job where even the most uninterested members of the family want to join in, and children love it.

Potatoes are often ready for harvesting from the time they begin to flower. Their flowers are purple or white, belonging to the nightshade family, and a reminder that though the tubers are edible, the rest of the plant is poisonous. Maincrop potatoes can be harvested after the haulms (the flowering stems and leaves) have died down. Dig them up on a dry, sunny day and leave them on the surface of the soil until their skins are quite dry. Before the sun starts to go down, drop them into double-thickness paper potato sacks and store them in a dry, frost-free place. "

Potatoes

Solanum tuberosum

Where would we be without the humble potato? We eat new potatoes with butter and mint in late spring and roast spuds when it is cold and dark outside; few weeks pass by without potatoes appearing on our plates in one form or another. To the vegetable gardener, they are an easy crop that can be relied upon. Digging up the tubers is a job that the everyone enjoys.

	J	F	M	A	M	J	J	A	S	O	N	D
Chit	■	■	■									
Plant			■	■	■							
Harvest						■	■	■	■	■	■	

Different types of potatoes

Potatoes come in a great diversity of sizes, shapes and colours, but they are classified as being either earlies or maincrops. Although both types should be planted at the same time, early types are ready to harvest much sooner than the maincrops, which tend to be larger and are the types that are stored over winter.

POTATO BLIGHT

Potato blight appears as brown blotches on the leaves and stems, and then affects the tubers, which soften, blacken, and smell dreadful. Quick action mitigates losses. Apply a copper-based fungicide or mancozeb, and cut off and bin or burn infected foliage to prevent spores washing down to the tubers. For the following year, choose a disease-resistant variety for future crops, such as 'Sarpo Mira' or 'Sarpo Axona'.

IT CAN TAKE four to six weeks for seed potatoes to sprout, after which they will be ready for planting.

You will also come across 'salad potatoes': these are either maincrop or early types that boil well and are particularly suitable served cold in salads.

The early group are what we call new potatoes. They are sub-divided into first earlies, which are ready to lift in just three months, and second earlies, which take a few weeks longer. New potatoes are always best when they are young and sweet, so a good technique is to grow just a few of each type. This avoids gluts of new potatoes you can't eat that will lose their sweetness over time.

Early potatoes are ideal for small plots, because they can be planted more closely together, and by the middle of summer they will all be dug, allowing you to transplant a different crop, such as beans or courgettes, into the same place. Maincrops occupy the ground for much longer.

The best sites and soils

Potatoes can be grown on almost any deep, well-drained soil in a sunny site. It certainly helps if the ground is fertile, so is you can, add plenty of well-rotted organic matter in the autumn of the year before. Just ahead of planting, you can dress the ground with a general fertilizer, and be sure to rake well to break up any large clods. Avoid waterlogged ground, low-lying spots where frosty air could collect – because potatoes are very susceptible to frost – and light, free-draining soil, which can result in drought and scab unless you choose drought-tolerant varieties. Also leave a gap of about three years before growing potatoes in the same spot to avoid the accumulation of soil-borne pest and diseases.

Small crops of potatoes can be grown in large containers. Placed in a warm, sunny place under cover, this is a good way of getting an early batch of new potatoes. With a bit of preparation, you could even have new potatoes in the middle of winter.

Sowing and planting

Getting potatoes started couldn't be easier. Just like in the supermarket, you buy potatoes off the shelf, but the difference is that the ones you need are special 'seed' potatoes – certifiably free from viruses. Usually they come in small bags, available from late winter, that may contain more potatoes than you need or have room to plant. In this case, share the purchase with a friend, or club in with others so that you can grow smaller quantities of a more diverse range of varieties. This way, you will discover much more quickly which varieties you prefer to eat, and which ones grow best in your soil.

Rather than eating your seed potatoes for dinner, you can start them into growth by sprouting or chitting them four to six weeks before planting. Set the tubers on end, with their 'eyes' uppermost, in egg boxes or seed trays, and place in good light in a cool room. Each potato will develop short green shoots, and the advantage of doing this is that it gets them into early growth, ready for the season ahead.

Begin planting your potatoes during early to late spring. You may want to get your earlies in first so that they crop sooner; another trick here is to increase the soil temperature with a covering of black plastic several weeks before planting, which accelerates growth. You can plant through holes made in the plastic.

The two methods of planting are to dig a trench or to plant in individual holes. Handle each sprouted

WHEN PLANTING OUT chitted potatoes, take care not to damage any of the delicate new shoots.

potato carefully, so that you do not knock off any of the shoots, and plant 15cm (6in) deep. Space 30cm (12in) apart, with 60cm (24in) between rows for earlies, and 40–75cm (16–30in) for maincrops. Closer planting often results in smaller potatoes at harvest time.

Alternatively, in a well-lit and ventilated, frost-free greenhouse or porch, plant into large 10-litre (2-gallon) tubs that are at least 30cm (12in) deep, with one chitted potato to a container half-filled with potting compost. Cover with 10cm (4in) of compost and top up as the plant grows.

Some rare varieties are not available as seed potatoes, but as virus-free microplants. These should be planted out as any other type of seedling, after the last frosts, to the same spacing.

Cultivating the crop

Outside, as soon as the first shoots emerge, start the process of earthing up by drawing up soil around and over them to produce a rounded ridge, repeating at one- to two-week intervals until the ridge is around 20–30cm (8–12in) high. This kills weeds, helps prevent blight, and prevents the tubers being exposed to the light and turning green and poisonous. You do not need to earth up potatoes growing under plastic sheeting. Cover shoots with soil or fleece if frost threatens. During dry spells, give the plants an

WHEN DIGGING UP potatoes, try to avoid spearing the tubers with your garden fork.

occasional but thorough watering to increase the yield. Plenty of water early on in the plants' development will lead to initiation of many tubers and a heavy crop later on.

Look out for potato blight, which is a problem in warm, wet summers, although early crops are not usually affected as they are harvested before blight can strike. Potato scab is less serious; it causes raised, scab-like lesions, but they are just superficial and are easily removed on peeling.

Soil-dwelling slugs are a nuisance as they eat and burrow into the tubers. Use of the biological control Nemaslug, which is applied to the soil during spring

and summer, can be effective. The presence of Colorado beetle is not common, but if you have it, it is often disastrous. Gardeners are required by law to notify the authorities. Plants that yellow, dry up and die from the bottom up may be showing signs of eelworm damage. These are quite common pests, and the best way to avoid them is to rotate your potato crop around the vegetable plot year after year and choose resistant varieties.

At harvest time

Lifting the first potatoes of the year is like digging up buried treasure. Choose a dry day. Earlies are ready when the flowers open or the buds drop, but first scrape away a little soil to check that they are large enough. Start lifting maincrops in late summer for immediate use. Carefully dig them up with a garden fork, taking care not to spear the tubers, and throw out any that are too small or excessively damaged or diseased, or have gone green through exposure to light – these are potentially harmful.

Small salad potatoes can be a bit fiddly to harvest. If you are intending to store the potatoes, leave them exposed to the air for a few hours so they can

Recommended varieties

Kestrel
A second early variety. This is a smooth-skinned potato with good slug resistance. Its versatility in the kitchen makes it a popular choice.

Accent
First early variety, with creamy waxy flesh and good scab and eelworm resistance. A very tasty new potato.

Lady Christl
A second early potato, long and oval in shape, with pale yellow skin, firm flesh and shallow eyes. It has good scab and eelworm resistance.

Picasso
An early maincrop variety. This is one of the heaviest-cropping potatoes, with creamy skin and striking bright red eyes. Resistant to eelworm and the common scab, it is good for dry soils.

IF YOUR GARDEN suffers badly from slugs, lift the potatoes as soon as they are ready.

dry off. Mildly damaged potatoes should be eaten promptly. You can leave maincrop potatoes in the ground, digging as you need them, but be aware that the longer you leave them there, the greater the chance of slug damage. Slugs make small holes in the skins and burrow their way into potatoes, often causing extensive damage. Some of your potatoes may have scabbing on the skins; it is not

serious and they just need to be peeled more deeply to remove the scabs. If the whole crop is affected, select a resistant variety to grow the following year.

Storing and cooking tips

Put your potatoes for storing into hessian or paper sacks and keep in a cool, dry, frost-free place until they are needed. Store only undamaged potatoes with any loose soil removed, and check the sacks regularly for signs of rot. Depending on how large your harvest, and how often you eat potatoes, the store may last you right through until early spring. As the weather warms up, your stored potatoes may start to sprout and shrivel, so finish them up.

With experience, you will find that different varieties of potato suit different types of cooking, and that others are not to your taste at all. Keep the largest potatoes for baking, and the smallest ones for boiling. Some varieties like the red-skinned 'Desirée', are great multi-purpose potatoes, and they are just as good baked as they are roasted, chipped, mashed or blended into soup. Knobbly potatoes can be a nuisance to clean, so you may want to give these a miss if you are short on preparation time.

Anya AGM
An excellent salad potato, with a pink/beige skin and waxy cream flesh. This potato has a lovely nutty flavour.

Cherie
A potato with a good yield; pink skinned, with yellow waxy flesh and a nice flavour.

Charlotte
A long oval variety, producing yellow skinned waxy potatoes with creamy yellow flesh. Excellent hot and cold in salads.

Dark Red Norland AGM
A heavy-cropping plant with dark red skin and pure white flesh. It has a good flavour for boiling and roasting.

Turnips
Brassica rapa (Rapifera Group)

Turnips should be harvested when fairly small and tasty; if they are allowed to get too old and large – beyond the size of a satsuma – you will find that they lose much of their appeal. An extra bonus of digging turnips when they are young is that you can also enjoy the fresh green leaves, or 'turnip tops', which have a peppery taste and can be added to salads or steamed.

	J	F	M	A	M	J	J	A	S	O	N	D
Sow		▪	▪	▪	▪	▪	▪					
Harvest				▪	▪	▪	▪	▪	▪	▪	▪	

The best sites and soils

Turnips perform best in cool climates with plenty of rainfall in an open, non-shaded site. The soil should be reasonably fertile and enriched with plenty of well-rotted organic matter before seeds are sown.

THIN OUT TURNIP SEEDLINGS to prevent overcrowding. They will need plenty of room to expand.

Sowing and planting

As for most root crops, turnips do not transplant well and must be directly sown outdoors where they are to grow. It is best to sow the crop in gradual succession over a number of months, so that gluts are avoided and you can continually harvest the emerging young plants.

Sowing can begin as early as late winter and continue right through to the end of summer, with at least two weeks between each sowing.

Seed should be sown thinly in 1cm (½in) deep rows; thin the emerging seedlings in stages until the plants are about 10–20cm (4–8in) apart. Hot, dry weather may stall the germination of turnip seeds, in which case the seedbed should be watered and lightly shaded with netting. Very early sowings may need to be protected from frost with fleece. The seedlings are especially vulnerable to slugs and snails at this stage.

Cultivating the crop

Water the developing plants every 5–10 days in dry spells to avoid irregular growth and splitting roots. Hoe or hand weed around the plants on a regular basis to keep them growing at their best. In summer, flea beetles can pepper the foliage with tiny holes, and this can be devastating. It will also mean that you won't be eating any of the turnip tops.

If flea beetles are a problem, cover the entire crop with horticultural fleece or very finely meshed netting secured firmly around the edges. If it is too late to prevent an infestation, badly affected plants can be dusted with derris powder.

As turnips are members of the cabbage family (see pages 68–91) they share many of the cultivation requirements as well as the same pests and diseases.

At harvest time

The roots will be ready in about six to ten weeks, depending on the variety grown, which means that the season for turnips runs from mid-spring well into autumn. Remember that turnips are not

HARVEST TURNIPS before the winter frosts and store them in a shallow box in a cool, frost-free place.

winter hardy, so they will need to be lifted before the cold weather really sets in.

A useful guide is to start pulling turnips when they reach the size of a golf ball, and do not let them develop any larger than a small orange, beyond which they become woody and much less tasty – check first by pulling back the foliage.

Storing and cooking tips

Like most veg, turnips are best fresh, but the late summer or autumn harvest can be stored in a cool, frost-free place; they will last longer if placed in a shallow box and covered with moist peat, coir compost or sand.

Recommended varieties

Primera AGM
Good yields of flat-topped roots with purple tops and attractive, smooth skin. It is best eaten when small and fresh.

Oasis
A good early crop of conical white turnips. It has very sweet flesh, which tastes of melon.

Swedes

Brassica napus (Napobrassica Group)

Also known as the Swedish turnip, because of its close relation to the less hardy turnip, the swede is grown solely for winter use. The crop can be left in the ground until mid-winter – useful for farmers growing them for animal fodder. The purple- or green-skinned roots are allowed to grow to a much larger size than turnips and have a yellow flesh that tastes milder and sweeter.

	J	F	M	A	M	J	J	A	S	O	N	D
Sow					▪	▪						
Harvest								▪	▪	▪	▪	▪

The best sites and soils

Swedes are normally grouped together with other plants of the cabbage family (see pages 68–91) because they share similar needs. They like to grow in full sun and well-drained, moisture-retentive soil, following a crop from the previous year that required the addition of plenty of organic matter, such as compost or well-rotted manure. This encourages

SWEDES GROW BEST in full sun, in soil that contains plenty of organic matter added the previous season.

strong growth and lessens the chances of the roots rotting over winter. Since swedes are prone to clubroot if grown on acid soil, check the pH of the soil and add a dressing of lime before sowing, if necessary, to increase the alkalinity. A moderate dressing of general-purpose fertilizer prior to sowing and planting is a good idea.

Sowing

Sow the seed directly into the prepared soil in late spring in northern or cold regions, or in early summer in warmer areas. Sow thinly in 1cm (½in) deep rows spaced 38cm (15in) apart. Thin the seedlings in stages until the plants are 23cm (9in) apart. In dry southern

districts, swedes may be easier to grow when raised in pots or trays as for other brassicas (see page 70).

Cultivating the crop

Like turnips, swedes share their cultivation needs and many of the pests and diseases of the cabbage family. Keep the crop well weeded so that the plants do not have to compete with other plants, and take precautions against pests like cabbage root fly, and flea beetle, by covering with fleece or finely meshed netting. Water the developing plants every 5–10 days in dry spells to avoid irregular growth and splitting roots, and to prevent powdery mildew forming on the leaves.

At harvest time

Swede roots can be harvested as soon as they are large enough to use – the larger the better. This may be as early as late summer, but since the plants take quite a long season to mature, up to seven or eight months, much depends on growing conditions, variety grown and time of sowing.

Harvest the roots as required over autumn and winter and into early spring; carefully pull or lift them from the soil, with a fork if necessary, and cut off the top growth. If you are really scraping around for food in early spring, and still have swedes in the ground, you can harvest the fresh young growth and serve it like cabbage.

SWEDES CAN BE USED to perk up all kinds of winter recipes, from casseroles to roasts. They can be stored in the ground or in cool, frost-free conditions.

Storing and cooking tips

For most varieties of swede, storage couldn't be easier. Up until early spring, simply leave the roots where they are growing in the ground until they are needed. Some varieties, however, can become woody if left in the ground beyond early winter, and should be lifted for storage before then. It's a good idea to check before you buy the seed.

Swedes lifted and stored in the same way as for turnips (see page 153), will be available when the ground is frozen solid and cannot be dug.

The buttery yellow flesh of swede (some are white) darkens to orange on cooking. All are an excellent source of vitamins, calcium and magnesium. Use the mild flavour in casseroles, or mashed with garlic and butter as part of a roast dinner. It also mashes well with other root crops, particularly carrots.

Recommended varieties

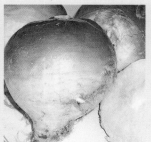

Magres AGM
A fairly round, good sized variety. It has sweet yellow flesh, contrasting with purple skin and powdery mildew-resistant foliage.

Ruby AGM
A swede with an elongated shape and good yellow flesh, bred for extra sweetness. The foliage is mildew-resistant.

Salads

Salads and leaves are surely the most rewarding crops to grow, especially if you want instant gratification. Play your cards right and you can pick fresh leaves every day of the year. Tasting delicious, they bear little resemblance to the pre-packed products on the supermarket shelves. Our ideas of what constitute a salad have changed radically over the past few years, and our salad horizons have been broadened to include mouth-watering shoots and leaves from all over the world. Some are colourful and textured enough to grow in the flowerbed; always grow a few extra for filling in gaps as they appear.

Salad leaves

"What a huge subject salad leaves is, and it's growing. A few years ago a British salad might have been a rather limited affair. Limp lettuce leaves, a few slices of soggy tomato and a radish. Distinctly unappetizing. Now all that has changed with the introduction of a huge range of unfamiliar leaves, roots, fruits and shoots.

Some old-fashioned lettuces, like 'Cos' and 'Webbs Wonderful' have a wonderful crunchy taste, but have to be picked whole when they are ready. Cut-and-come-again have taken over, offering delicious leaves over a period of months. And constantly picking leaves from the likes of 'Salad Bowl' and 'Oak Leaf', rather than lifting the whole plant, keeps them immature. Consequently two or three sowings should last a whole summer, right into autumn.

Decorative pots or containers make excellent 'gardens' for cut-and-come-again crops, but lettuce is just the start of it. There are a host of other salad

YOU CAN'T BEAT a trip to the vegetable garden, picking your own fresh salad, and mixing the colours, tastes and textures.

leaves – chicory, endive, claytonia, sorrel and spinach – that can be used in this way. Rocket has become a regular item on supermarket shelves, but leaves straight from the garden with a drizzle of olive oil and shaved Parmesan is another experience. And of course eating fresh leaves full of vitamins and minerals is the best possible diet.

One of the best salads is a good mesclun mix. Mesclun has no essential ingredients but, as it has always been understood in France, is an elegant mixture of young leaves, according to what is available, but always perfectly balanced so that no one ingredient dominates. The contents may be any or all of the following: baby lettuce, rocket, lamb's lettuce, endive and chervil. Keeping to the spirit of mesclun, a modern mix might include other leaves, perhaps Chinese and Japanese mustards, mizuna and mibuna. All are fast-growing and have various degrees of heat. Although many mustards run to seed very quickly, mizuna and mibuna do not. Just pick them regularly to maintain fresh supplies."

Lettuces *Lactuca sativa*

The range of lettuces on sale in supermarkets is so small that you could be forgiven for thinking that there are no other varieties. Not so. There are scores to choose from, each with its own flavour, texture and colour. Some are colourful and textured enough to grow in the flowerbed.

	J	F	M	A	M	J	J	A	S	O	N	D
Sow			▪	▪	▪	▪	▪	▪	▪			
Harvest					▪	▪	▪	▪	▪	▪	▪	▪

Different types of lettuces

Lettuces can be divided into two main kinds: hearting lettuces, which produce a dense centre; and loose-leaf types with a more open arrangement of leaves. A big advantage of growing loose-leaf lettuces is that you can just cut a few leaves at a time, whereas hearting lettuces are generally harvested whole.

Hearting Crisphead, or iceberg lettuces have wavy outer leaves and crisp pale hearts. Although crispheads add a refreshing crunch to salads, they can be low on flavour, and are best combined with other leaves. Cos lettuces are distinguished by their upright leaves. A semi-Cos is smaller, denser and sweet-tasting, the best-known being 'Little Gem'. Butterhead lettuces, as the name implies, have soft, tender leaves. They will quickly wilt after cutting

PLANTS LEFT TOO LONG after maturing will run to seed or 'bolt', and go on to flower.

unless they are plunged into water, but the hearts have excellent flavour.

Loose-leaf They have highly decorative leaf shapes, including curled and frilly-leaved 'lollo' or 'salad bowl' types, and striking 'oak leaf' varieties. There are many beautiful red-leaved varieties, some of which can have a slightly bitter taste.

The best sites and soils

Lettuce is easy to grow, but needs conditions that allow it to grow quickly or the leaves develop a bitter taste. Grow in full sun on moisture-retentive, reasonably fertile soil. Early and late sowings may need protecting against the cold.

Sowing and planting

For summer crops, sow seed outdoors from mid-spring to late summer, thinly, in drills 1cm (½in) deep. Since germination can be erratic in hot weather, sow seed in the afternoon so that it will germinate in the cool of the night. For autumn crops, sow in late

BOLTING LETTUCES

Lettuce is an annual that matures in weeks and then bolts. The time between reaching maturity and bolting is partly governed by environmental factors; hot, dry weather encourages bolting, but all varieties react differently. Loose-leaf, Cos and many crisphead kinds usually take the longest time, the butterheads being quickest. To help prevent bolting, mulch around plants and water during dry weather. Lettuce that has gone to seed is often bitter, but will produce a cascade of foliage and flowers if left.

SOWING LETTUCE IN SMALL SPACES

1 YOU CAN GROW a wide range of lettuce leaves in gaps in containers or raised beds. Make drills for sowing the seed.

2 SOW THE SEED from mid-spring to late summer. Thinnings from the crop as it germinates can be eaten as baby leaves.

3 WATER IN well and ensure the seedlings get plenty of sunlight. Regularly water – during hot, dry weather – and weed.

summer and early autumn, protecting plants with cloches or fleece as temperatures cool. Final spacings in the row will be from 15cm–30cm (6–12in), depending on the variety; see the seed packet for individual instructions. Thinned seedlings can usually be transplanted, provided this is done in cool weather and plants are well watered afterwards; replanting the seedlings amongst slow-maturing crops like brassicas is an effective use of space. Thinnings can also be eaten. Alternatively, rows of seeds can be sown more densely a as cut-and-come-again crop. Sow successionally, throughout summer.

Cultivating the crop

Keep lettuces well watered. Feed only if growth is poor, using a nitrogen-rich fertilizer.

At harvest time

Harvest lettuces by cutting rather than pulling; the stems will often sprout fresh leaves if cut off close to ground level, provided conditions are not too hot and dry. Loose-leaf types are particularly good at this, and leaving a few of the outer leaves will help the plant to re-establish itself.

Recommended varieties

Little Gem AGM
A variety of Cos lettuce with small solid heads of mid green, medium-blistered leaves. It has a sweet, crisp heart. Resistant to root aphid.

Clarion AGM
An fairly open-headed butterhead lettuce that can be grown for spring or autumn cropping under protection. Good quality with some mildew resistance.

Sangria AGM
A butterhead variety for summer cropping with soft, pale green, pink tipped leaves. It is slow to mature and resistant to bolting.

Tom Thumb
A small and solid lettuce of the butterhead type, with soft leaves and a mild taste. It crops early and is suitable for growing in restricted spaces.

THE MORE YOU PICK, the more the plants grow tasty replacement leaves.

Cut-and-come-again crops should be harvested when about 10cm (4in) high.

In hot weather, harvest in the morning, putting small leaves of a cut-and-come-again salad straight into a bucket of clean water to prevent wilting. Many varieties will store well in the fridge for a couple of days at least in a polythene bag, if wetted first, but wash again before use.

Pests and diseases

There are four main potential problems. Firstly, slugs and snails demolishing seedlings. Second, young plants wilting overnight, probably because they've had their roots attacked by cutworms or chafer grubs in the soil. Fork through the soil to expose and get rid of any pests.

Third, when older plants suddenly wilt and die back, usually in mid- and late summer, they've almost certainly suffered from an infestation of lettuce root aphid. Pull up any affected plants – they usually come out easily because the roots have been eaten – and dispose of them. Avoid growing more lettuces in the same site and, if the problem is persistent, try resistant varieties such as 'Avondefiance'. And fourth, grey mould or botrytis may be a problem in cold, damp summers. To prevent these attacks, increase the spacing between the plants and remove any infected material immediately.

Lobjoit's Green Cos AGM
A large Cos variety with an open head and relatively smooth mid-green leaves. It has crisp, tasty leaves.

Bijou AGM
A leafy Batavian lettuce with attractive red glossy leaves and a good flavour. The plants are uniform with a fairly small frame.

Set AGM
A crisphead variety, this lettuce is easy to grow and slow to bolt. It is medium to large in size, solid and heavy with crisp green leaves.

Lollo Rossa Assor AGM
A hardy, slow to bolt leafy lettuce with attractive pale green red-tipped leaves. It has a distinctive peppery taste.

OTHER VARIETIES OF SALAD LEAVES

Buckler-Leaved Sorrel
A perennial herb with bright green arrow-shaped leaves with a sharp lemony flavour. Use sparingly to perk up a salad. Sorrel self-seeds quite readily, and it is worth saving a few new plants to replace the parent which can develop a woody centre fairly rapidly.

Red Orach
This rapid-growing hardy annual has arrowhead-shaped leaves of deep maroon-red. It bolts quickly forming bushy plants with tall, attractive seedheads. It is therefore necessary to make a number of successional sowings because the young leaves are the most tender and have the best colour. Initially sow seed in shallow drills, and thereafter allow to self-seed or collect seed for re-use.

Corn Salad
Corn salad, or lamb's lettuce, forms rosettes of small, bright green, succulent leaves. It is very hardy and can withstand frost. Although it will stop putting on new growth in very cold weather, it is a good source of salad over winter and in early spring before it runs to seed. Sow seed in shallow drills in late summer or early autumn for a winter crop, and then sow again in early spring for a second crop.

Rocket
The leaves have a distinctive peppery taste. Sow successively from early spring until very late summer, in shallow drills. Harvest as a cut-and-come-again crop, snipping them off with scissors when about 15cm (6in) high. In the height of summer rocket will bolt rapidly, the leaves becoming tough and coarse. Wild or Turkish rocket are more bolt-resistant than leaf rocket; they have a different flavour but are still delicious.

Edible flowers and herbs

People are often surprised to discover that flowers can be used in the kitchen. Some flower petals have a strong peppery or fruity taste, while others impart more subtle aromas and flavours. Some simply look exquisite, and are therefore fun to use. They can be scattered in salads, frozen in ice cubes, crystallised or used to flavour biscuits and ice creams.

Preparing and collecting flowers

Growing a few edible flowers amongst your vegetables will often reap other rewards. Many of the flowers that are best for this use also make excellent companion plants or attract pollinating insects to the plot. Some of the more vigorous annuals like nasturtium act like green manures, suppressing weeds and reducing evaporation of moisture from the soil's surface.

Flowers wilt quickly, especially in hot weather, so pick in the morning where possible. Take care not to get stung by bees, particularly when picking borage, lavender and chives. Pick whole flowerheads rather than petals, then go indoors where it is cooler to prepare them. Spread the flowers out on a piece of kitchen towel as you work; this will allow any small black pollen beetles to be easily removed as they move between flowers. In most species, the flowers are too tough to consume whole and the petals should be removed from the flowerhead or calyx by gently pulling them away. Put the prepared petals or flower heads into a small polythene bag and seal it with a little air inside to stop the contents getting squashed. The flowers should keep like this in the fridge for several hours.

Avoid washing flowers as most are easily damaged, but if they are wilting, put the heads in a bowl of water to revive them.

Annual flowers

Annual flowers are the easiest to include in a vegetable plot because they are short-lived. Most of those recommended also self-seed readily, so you

A FLOWERY SALAD

1 TREAT THE FLOWERS with care. First, remove them whole, letting any insects escape. Then nip off the petals and add to a salad, or briefly store in a polythene bag in a fridge.

2 A LIVELY MIX of edible flowers and leaves give a salad an extra peppery, fruity, nutty taste. Possible ingredients include nasturtiums, calendula and tagetes.

Calendula (*Calendula officinalis*) – A hardy annual with double and single varieties in shades of orange. Dead head to prolong flowering or use successional sowings. Petals add colour to salads.

Nasturtium (*Tropaeolum majus*) – Both the leaves and petals have a strong peppery taste which takes a few seconds to develop on the tongue. Flower colour can vary from deep red to butter yellow. The fresh seed heads can be collected and pickled to use as capers.

should have to buy only one packet of seed to get started. Sow in drills and take note of what the seedlings look like so that you know not to weed them out in subsequent years. Inevitably, self-seeded plants will appear in the wrong place, but these can easily be transplanted.

Aromatic herbs

The flowers of many aromatic herbs, both annual and perennial, retain the flavour of the leaves but with less intensity, making them perfect for adding to salads. Dill, coriander and rocket are annuals that can be used in this way when they run to seed, using whole flowers. The flower heads of chives, garlic chives and lavender are composed of lots of smaller individual flowers which can be snipped off with a pair of scissors and then eaten whole. Lavender flowers can be used to flavour biscuits, cakes and ice cream. The intensity of flavour can vary significantly from plant to plant, so it is worth experimenting with quantities. Sage petals can also be used.

Perennial flowers

If you get the taste for edible flowers, there are numerous garden flowers that can supplement your harvest. Try roses, hemerocallis and sweet bergamot for flavour, and primulas for decoration.

Courgette flowers

The Greeks use courgette flowers to create a tasty starter by stuffing them with a piece of feta cheese, dipping them in batter and quick-frying them. The intense yellow of the flower is revealed only when you bite into the parcels of cheese.

PICK LARGE BATCHES of lavender flowers just as they open, and the leaves at any time, to use in a wide range of recipes including biscuits and ice cream.

Tagetes (*Tagetes tenuifolia*) – The bush marigold ('Lemon Gem', 'Tangerine Gem') does not self-seed very reliably, but young plants are available from garden centres and is very easy to raise from seed. The petals have a distinctive zesty flavour.

Heartsease (*Viola tricolor*) – This delicate wildflower is small enough to use whole. Just snip as much of the calyx off as is possible without causing it to fall apart. It is particularly pretty frozen in ice cubes and used in summer drinks. Cultivated violas and pansies can also be used but are best bought as bedding plants. Winter flowering pansies will provide a useful supply of flowers when little else is available.

Clary Sage (*Salvia sclarea*) – Strictly speaking it is not the flowers that are of interest here but the purple and pink bracts. Select the younger ones as these are brighter and will not yet have become papery. Their flavour is negligible but they make a decorative garnish.

Borage (*Borago officinalis*) – This is a tall bushy plant up to a metre (or yard) high and apt to flop without some support, so make sure you have allowed enough room for it. The blue starry flowers are easily detached from the hairy calyx by gently pulling at the centre of the flower. They look particularly beautiful in ice cubes or mixed with dark-leafed lettuce. The young leaves have a refreshing cucumber-like flavour and can be added chopped to summer drinks.

Chicory
Cichorium intybus

Chicory tolerates damp summers well and some varieties, if given protection, are hardy enough to be grown through winter for a spring harvest. There are three main types: witloof (Belgian), radicchio (red), and sugarloaf. They make elegant plants for the vegetable border and can be grown among ornamentals. Witloof chicory can be forced to produce white leafy buds called chicons.

	J	F	M	A	M	J	J	A	S	O	N	D
Sow				▪	▪	▪	▪	▪				
Plant					▪	▪						
Harvest					▪	▪	▪	▪	▪	▪		

The best sites and soils

Chicory grows best on a light soil with a reasonable amount of organic matter mixed in to keep the soil moist. Although chicory grows happily in full sun, it doesn't mind a bit of shade, which makes the vegetables ideal for growing between taller crops.

Sowing and planting

Sow the seeds from mid-spring to summer, either directly into the ground, or in modules under warmer conditions for later planting. The latter method is usually preferred, since germination can often be quite patchy, and it also helps to prevent bolting (where the plant makes flowers instead of leaves), which is a problem in cool spring weather. Later sowings are less likely to bolt and can be harvested well into autumn, and since the leaves can stand a small degree of frost, chicory makes a useful late salad crop. Take care when transplanting the seedlings because they don't respond well to root disturbance. Space plants 35cm (14in) apart.

As an alternative to cropping whole plants, chicory grows well as a cut-and-come-again crop, especially the sugarloaf types.

Cultivating the crop

Chicory has the appearance of lettuce and grows extremely quickly, so it is not affected by many pests and diseases, apart from the usual suspects: slugs, snails and the occasional caterpillar. The plants also have a habit of bolting, particularly if the soil dries out or if the plants were started too early in spring; after midsummer it seldom disappoints.

Witloof chicory forms a loose rosette with a deep root, and radicchio and sugarloaf types both usually form hearts of leaves, although a proportion of any crop will always fail to do so. Water plants during dry weather and apply a nitrogen-rich fertilizer if growth begins to flag.

The bitter taste of chicory is sometimes welcome in salads, but it can be removed by steaming, gentle boiling, or, best of all, by blanching, where light is excluded from parts of the plant. On open-hearted types, the best method is to cover the entire centre of the plant with a plate, which allows some light to reach the outer leaves and leads to an attractive

CHICORY ADDS a sharp, colourful Italian touch to salads. If the taste is slightly on the bitter side, and children might complain, the leaves can be steamed, blanched or boiled.

TO GET A GRADATION of colours from green at the leaf tips to white at the base, grow a self-blanching radicchio or sugarleaf type. Tie the leaves together, to increase the effect.

TO BLANCH the entire plant, exclude the light by covering with a bucket. This should take approximately 10 days. Don't leave for too long or it will deteriorate.

gradation from green to white. To blanch the whole plant, cover it with a bucket.

As radicchio and sugarloaf types both form a heart, they are self-blanching; to enhance this, tie the leaves together. Blanch only as many plants as you are likely to need, as the plants will start to deteriorate if left covered for too long. It should take about ten days for blanching to take place.

When forced, the deep roots of witloof chicory produce chicons. To force these outdoors without having to dig up the roots, cut off the leafy head to leave a 5cm (2in) stub. Use a hoe to draw soil over these stubs, and within a few weeks, chicons will form under the soil, particularly if a cloche is used to provide extra warmth. Better results are often achieved by forcing indoors, where plants are lifted and planted in a box of moist peat or peat substitute, with the leaves trimmed to 1cm (½in) from the roots. Cover the roots with 23cm (9in) more peat and put the box in a warm, dark place. Modern witloof varieties may need darkness only to form chicons.

At harvest time

Cut blanched plants immediately, as once the cover is removed, the plants will start to revert to their dark green colouring and bitter taste. The leaves have better keeping properties than lettuce once cut, if stored in a cool place. Chicons will be ready for eating about one month after being covered.

Recommended varieties

Palla Rossa AGM
A classic red radicchio with large head and well-filled red heart, good for colourful autumn salads. It needs cold temperatures before it turns red. Bolt-resistant.

Pan di Zucchero AGM
A very well known sugarloaf chicory with upright green leaves and a long, dense heart. The centre of the plant responds well to blanching.

Cucumbers *Cucumis sativus*

The fresh taste and crunchy texture of any home-grown cucumber will amply demonstrate the shortcomings of its shop-bought cousin. Though the smoothest used to be grown under cover, newer outdoor varieties have long, smooth fruit with excellent flavour. Older, outdoor types with smaller, almost prickly shapes, known as ridge cucumbers, are also worth growing.

	J	F	M	A	M	J	J	A	S	O	N	D
Sow			▪	▪	▪							
Plant				▪	▪	▪						
Harvest						▪	▪	▪	▪			

The best sites and soils

Cucumbers need plenty of sun, moisture and good soil, with a dressing of general purpose fertilizer. They thrive in large pots (minimum 10 litres), in growbags or in the ground. Containers need to be filled with rich, fresh potting compost, and beds need plenty of well-rotted organic matter. To avoid a build-up of pests and diseases, grow both kinds in a different site every year, or in containers.

INDOOR CUCUMBERS need careful planting. Water the container prior to planting, then plant so that the seedling is proud of the soil. Try not to water again until well rooted.

SUPPORTING CUCUMBERS

Greenhouse cucumbers and some outdoor types need support in the form of canes or netting that should be erected before planting. Tie in shoots regularly, pinch out the growing tip once the plant reaches the top of its support, and pinch out lateral shoots when there are two leaves. Outdoor varieties can be allowed to trail without support; the main shoot should be pinched at five to six leaves to encourage branching, and black plastic should be spread beneath to protect the crop.

Sowing and planting

Although greenhouse cucumbers can be sown direct, you'll get a longer harvest by starting off seed in late winter or early spring, though you could buy ready-grown plants in spring and early summer. Allow four to five weeks from sowing to planting. In a greenhouse heated to a constant minimum temperature of 21°C (70°F), plant from early spring, while in an unheated greenhouse, sow in late spring. Put the large seeds, singly on edge to prevent rotting, 1cm (½in) deep in small pots of moist seed compost, and place in a warm spot (a heated propagator is ideal). Grow on a sunny windowsill or in a heated greenhouse. Be careful not to overwater and, once the first true leaves have expanded, move to 13cm (5in) pots. Outdoor varieties are best started indoors in late spring, sowing three seeds in a small pot. In warm areas, sow three seeds 2cm (¾in) deep where the cucumbers are to grow. Thin to one plant when big enough to handle and plant out pots as soon as the rootball holds together. Be careful to plant in moist soil and avoid soil touching the base of the stem. Not only will cloches of fleece increase soil temperatures, but they will also greatly boost growth and yield.

Cultivating the crop

Water regularly, adding a general liquid feed if plants fail to thrive. Once the crop starts to swell, feed weekly with tomato fertilizer. Under cover, spray the ground with water on hot days to boost humidity.

At harvest time

Once the cucumbers are sufficiently large, cut them off using a sharp knife, and pick before the strongest heat of the day for maximum crispness. Harvest regularly, because leaving mature cucumbers on the plant will stop the development of new ones.

Pests and diseases

Check regularly under covers for pests and diseases and choose disease-resistant varieties. The most troublesome is powdery mildew – a dusty white covering on the leaves. Sulphur dust can limit damage but discard badly affected plants. Combat red spider mite and whitefly with biological controls.

HARVEST when fruit tips are rounded with parallel sides and no longer pointed.

Recommended varieties

Masterpiece AGM
A fairly short but straight, smooth-skinned, dark green cucumber with excellent texture and flavour. Good for growing in the open garden.

Carmen AGM
A heavy-cropping variety with excellent disease resistance. The fruit are of average length, dark green and slightly ribbed.

Marketmore AGM
This variety gives a large yield of short, slightly spiny, dark green fruits. It has good disease resistance and can be grown in the open garden or large containers and growbags.

Long Green Ridge
A heavily cropping variety with dark green fruits. These are large cucumbers, slightly bumpy in appearance, and excellent for use in salads.

Radishes

Raphanus sativus

Summer radish is an easily grown, hardy vegetable that adds crunch and spiciness to salads. It is fast-growing, usually maturing in about four weeks. The roots may be red, pink or white, and pointed, cylindrical or round. A small number of varieties are grown for their crunchy seedpods, eaten raw. The large winter and Oriental radishes are excellent winter vegetables.

	J	F	M	A	M	J	J	A	S	O	N	D
Sow			▪	▪	▪	▪	▪	▪				
Harvest	▪				▪	▪	▪	▪	▪	▪	▪	▪

The best sites and soils

Radishes need fertile, moisture-retentive soil. Avoid dry conditions when they might well run to seed or produce tough, pithy or hot, peppery-tasting roots. In the height of summer, radish may grow better in the partial shade of other crops.

Sowing and planting

Radish can be sown from early spring until early autumn. For early and late sowings, use early varieties and cover with a cloche or a layer of fleece. Sow seed thinly, in drills 1cm (½in) deep that have been watered beforehand. Thin the seedlings to at least 3cm (1⅛in) apart, or the overcrowding makes them spindly and may delay or prevent the roots from developing fully.

Radishes, being fast growers, are ideally suited to a number of small successional sowings throughout

SOWING SMALL SEED means you'll inevitably end up with rows of tightly packed seedlings, but they can easily be thinned.

MARKING OUT OTHER CROPS

Radish can be used as a 'marker' for slow-to-germinate crops such as parsnips, to prevent the slower-growing seed rows from being accidentally disturbed while weeding. Sow alternate pinches of seed so that the radish can be pulled up without disturbing the parsnips.

the season, and can be grown amongst slower-maturing crops and to fill gaps where a couple of lettuces or a few beetroots have been harvested.

Radish can also be grown as a cut-and-come-again crop for its spicy leaves. Summer radish is best harvested when it's still small and tender.

Cultivating the crop

Water regularly in dry weather to prevent plants from bolting or becoming woody. Irregular watering can result in splitting, while lush, leafy growth may be caused by overwatering.

At harvest time

Pull up radishes as soon as they are mature. They do not last well in the ground, but will store for several days in the fridge if they are first rinsed, patted dry and placed in a polythene bag. Use sliced or grated in salads and sandwiches.

Pests and diseases

Radishes are prone to flea beetle attacks which create numerous small holes in the leaves. Damage is often superficial, but attacks can be prevented by covering the seedlings with fleece or very fine plastic mesh, sold as flea beetle-proof. Seedlings are also at risk from slugs and snails, and from the cabbage root fly whose larvae feed on the roots. Any damage is more likely to occur the longer radish is in the ground.

Alternative radishes

Winter Radish A much hardier black form, it is harvested in late autumn or winter. It generally forms larger roots than summer radish, but it can be used in the same way. Direct sowing is restricted to mid- to late summer. Earlier sowings are likely to bolt, while later sowings may not put on enough growth before cooler weather arrives. Winter radishes can be left in the ground providing it is reasonably well drained and they are protected from any severe frosts, which means that one sowing in late summer is necessary. Sow as for summer radish, but thin to 10cm (4in) apart, in rows 25cm (10in) apart. Harvest from the late autumn, through the winter.

Oriental Radish This large-rooted radish may be round or semi-round with red, green or white flesh, and can be eaten raw, stir-fried or cooked. It has a

HARVEST RADISHES by taking hold of the top growth and easing them out with a fork, trowel or even a plastic plant label. Don't leave them in the ground for too long when mature.

different texture and flavour to a summer radish. The mooli radish has long, white, cylindrical roots. Some of the mooli radishes, such as 'Long White Icicle', can also be eaten when immature, as a summer radish. Sow as for winter radish, and thin to 20–30cm (8–12in) apart depending on the variety. Plants will take at least eight weeks to mature, but last well left in the ground.

Recommended varieties

Marabelle AGM
Small-leaved variety with early, round, small and bright red roots. Tasty and easy to grow.

French Breakfast 3 AGM
Cylindrical variety; red with a white tip. Initially has a mild taste but will become hot if left in the ground.

Sparkler AGM
The medium-sized roots are slightly flattened with a white base. They grow reliably and easily, and mature quickly.

Scarlet Globe AGM
A fast-growing radish with deep red roots and crisp white flesh. It is very well regarded and widely grown.

Tomatoes

" Imagine the banks of a Peruvian river, swathed in mist, the temperature warm and even. Perfect conditions for tomatoes. This is where most of the tomato species come from, including their direct descendants which we grow and eat today.

Surprisingly, the tomato hasn't always been popular. It was largely ignored in Peru where it grew wild, but travelled one way and another to New Mexico, where it's believed to have become a food crop from around AD 400. The Aztecs grew it and, in the 16th century, it was brought to Spain along with the potato, aubergine and maize. When Napoli fell under Spanish rule a few years later, it made its debut in what was to become Italy.

Gradually tomatoes found their way around Europe, and were recorded in

YOU CAN'T BEAT the taste and tangy aroma of shiny, fresh tomatoes straight from the vine, sliced into a summer salad.

Gerard's Herbal as 'love apples'. The tomato was commonly regarded as an aphrodisiac, which is why it was also called pomme d'amour and pomum amoris, now pomodoro. It was also viewed in some circles with suspicion and disdain because of its similarity to the highly toxic nightshade, and to mandrake which, legend has it, screams if you pull it out of the ground.

Eventually taste overcame doubt, and it is now the most researched vegetable or fruit. Tomatoes are good for you and, although they can be very acidic, they are packed with vitamins A and C. In the United Kingdom, almost all commercial tomatoes are grown under glass. They need heat to be successful. If you choose outdoor varieties, start them off early and give them the hottest spot you've got, and they should crop with good yields. The Chinese grow 20 million tonnes of tomatoes a year.

My mum always used to grow a few tomatoes. 'Golden Sunrise' and 'Gardener's Delight' were her favourites for their taste but also because of their ability to ripen well. And when you're growing your own fruit and vegetables, taste is what counts. Supermarkets are interested only in reliability, uniformity and shelf-life.

When we had our first greenhouse here, I grew tomatoes and our eldest daughter, Annie, quickly developed a passion for them. Their ripening coincided with her first steps, and she would make her way to the greenhouse only to be discovered minutes later with her cheeks stuffed with them. **"**

Tomatoes

Lycopersicon esculentum

Well before you embark on tomato growing, you are bound to know whether you will be growing them outdoors or under the protection of a greenhouse. This is a fundamental matter: your chances of success are slim if you try to grow an indoor type outside. If you get it right, you are likely to be picking tomatoes into the dying days of summer, relishing those last fruity drops of sunshine before autumn kicks in.

	J	F	M	A	M	J	J	A	S	O	N	D
Sow		▪	▪	▪								
Plant*				▪	▪							
Harvest*							▪	▪	▪	▪		

Different types of tomatoes

As an indicator of their popularity, hundreds of tomato varieties are available to gardeners, which can make for a lifetime of experimentation. The fruits vary from tiny cherry tomatoes to the giant beefsteaks, from yellow to red to purple, and they may be round, flattened or elongated. Taste can range from fairly insipid to sweet or richly flavoured. Not all types grow well outdoors, so check before buying. The plants themselves are either vines or bushes. Vines are ideal for greenhouses but need the help of a support to grow, whereas bush types are more compact and can be left to their own devices. Varieties bred for hanging baskets and containers make compact growth. Some varieties, particularly old-fashioned ones, show both bush and vine characteristics.

The best sites and soils

Tomatoes can be grown under cover, out of doors, and even in hanging baskets and window boxes. Tomatoes that are growing in a greenhouse, conservatory and even a porch will fruit earlier and for longer, particularly if the first two are heated, but even a cheap polythene tunnel will help keep your tomatoes snug and speed up ripening. When growing plants in the open, a sunny, sheltered site is essential, such as against a sunny wall. Fertile soil is also vital, and tomatoes do best in growbags, or large containers

GROWING CORDON or upright tomatoes in pots. Terracotta is a good choice because the pots are heavy and unlikely to get blown over. Note the need for canes to train the growth up.

GROWING MARIGOLDS with tomatoes in a greenhouse apparently keeps away swarms of greenfly, with the strong marigold smell repelling the pests, or acting as a magnet.

PLANTING TOMATOES IN GROWBAGS

1 PLACE THE BAG in a sunny position and cut two slits to form a cross in the plastic, peeling it back to expose the compost.

2 SPACE THE SLITS about 45cm (18in) apart. Don't try to pack the plants any closer together or they'll shade each other.

3 MAKE HOLES in the compost and gently ease in each seedling (they should usually be sturdier than shown and beginning to form their first flowers).

4 CONTINUE PLANTING, taking care not to damage any roots and stems, and then water in. Fix strong supports above the plants, to which the new growth can be attached.

of fresh potting compost. Plants growing in the ground will thrive provided the soil has been enriched with plenty of well-rotted organic matter and tomato fertilizer. However, if tomatoes are likely to occupy the same site for several years, as in a greenhouse bed, growing in containers or bags is best otherwise pests and diseases are likely to build up in the soil.

Sowing and planting

Sturdy plants need plenty of light. Space them so the leaves do not touch in the brightest place you can find. If they do get leggy, plant them deeply. Since tomatoes are sensitive to frost, they can be planted out only once all risk of frost has passed. Sow seeds thinly, about eight weeks before planting time, in a pot or tray of moist seed compost. Cover lightly with

a layer of seed compost, place the container in a polythene bag (with a label if you're growing more than one variety), and put it in a warm place, such as an airing cupboard. Wait several days and then check daily for signs of germination. Once shoots emerge, move the container to a warm, well-lit spot and let the seedlings grow. Pot up them individually into 8cm (3in) pots as soon as they are large enough to handle, and keep the potting compost evenly moist.

Tomatoes usually germinate easily and you are likely to have plenty of seedlings, so keep a few as spares in case of emergencies and throw out or give away the rest. Plant out the young tomato plants when they are around 15–23cm (6–9in) tall, spacing them 45cm (18in) apart. In a greenhouse heated to 18°C (64°F), planting can be done from mid-February; in an

BIOLOGICAL CONTROL

Plants growing under glass are susceptible to whitefly and red spider mite. The former initially look like airborne specks of white dust, but close inspection under the leaves and a quick tap, sending scores flying away, immediately indicates the problem. The biological control *Encarsia formosa*, a tiny parasitic wasp, is available to use against whitefly. Pots of marigolds or basil planted beside the tomatoes is said to help; either because the strong smell keeps whitefly at bay, or the whitefly prefer the strong-smelling plants and target those instead; however it is supposed to work, it is not a proven control, although there is no harm trying. Red spider mite infestations can be spotted if the leaves develop a silvery sheen and fine silky white webs start appearing around the leaves and stems. Apart from misting the air regularly, you can try the biological control *Phytoseiulus persimilis*, a predatory mite. Biological controls can be very effective indeed if introduced early enough.

unheated covered environment, begin in mid-spring; outside, wait until early summer. Vine tomatoes need to be trained against canes, string, or a proprietary support, and ideally this should be in place before planting. Plant three trailing tomatoes to each medium to large hanging basket or window box.

Cultivating the crop

Tomatoes are thirsty and hungry plants, and the soil should be kept evenly moist. Avoid fluctuations between wet and dry, which results in the fruit splitting, and dry conditions can cause blossom end rot when part of the fruit becomes blackened. Also feed regularly using a specific tomato fertilizer, according to the manufacturer's instructions. Bush and trailing tomatoes need little attention, but vine types need to be tied in regularly and their side shoots need snapping or cutting off, which concentrates the plants' energy on the fruit that grow from the main stem. Remove any yellowing lower leaves as they appear. Potato blight can be devastating on outdoor crops, turning leaves then stems and fruit black and ultimately killing the plants. Early treatment may be effective, by removing and

Recommended varieties

Sungold
An exceptionally sweet, orange-red cherry tomato that does best if given some protection. The growth is vine-type and has some virus resistance.

Golden Sunrise AGM
These unusual, small yellow, medium-sized tomatoes are borne on vine-type plants. They make colourful additions to summer salads and have a nice fruity flavour.

Gold Nugget AGM
A very tasty cherry tomato of bush habit. The fruits are a shade of golden yellow and are early to crop with good yields.

Tornado AGM
Does well in containers and in the ground; can be supported with short stakes or allowed to sprawl. Bushy habit.

PICK TOMATOES when fully ripe and evenly coloured, but don't leave them too long or they will split. You can ripen green fruit on a windowsill.

destroying infected leaves and by spraying with a copper-based fungicide or mancozeb, but there is little you can do once the disease takes hold. Under glass, tomatoes sometimes suffer from whitefly, aphids and red spider mite. Biological controls are very effective against all these pests if introduced early enough (see box opposite). Use a sticky yellow trap to give early warning of problems. Oil- or soap-based insecticides are fairly effective in reducing pest numbers to allow biological controls to overcome pests. Diseases are usually avoided if ventilation is used to keep the air and the plants dry.

At harvest time

Pick the fruit when fully ripe and evenly coloured, but don't leave mature fruit on the plant for long or it'll soften and split. At the end of the season, outdoor and unheated greenhouse plants are likely to be left with lots of green fruit. This can be picked and ripened on a sunny windowsill or in a drawer along with a couple of ripe apples or bananas, which give off the ripening gas ethylene.

Storing and cooking tips

If tomatoes are stored in the fridge, take them out early and serve at room temperature for the best flavour. Surplus fruit can be made into sauces.

Outdoor Girl AGM
An early ripening variety that will grow well outdoors. The vine-type growth produces trusses of classic round red tomatoes that have a good flavour.

Gardener's Delight AGM
Vine-type cherry tomatoes with an exceptionally sweet flavour. The plants bear long trusses of fruit and will grow either under glass or outside in a warm spot.

Olivade AGM
The large, dark red plum tomatoes are very early to mature and are borne in profusion on the vine-type growth. They are juicy and fruity with a good flavour. For outdoors or under glass.

Summer Sweet AGM
Expect heavy crops of attractive small red, juicy plum tomatoes. They are very early to mature. For outdoors or under glass.

Spinach and chard

Spinach and chard are stalwarts of the vegetable garden and will keep you in green, leafy vegetables almost all year round. They are highly adaptable, and the leaves can be harvested when small as a cut-and-come-again crop for salads, or be allowed to grow larger for cooking. They are particularly rich in iron and a good source of folic acid. Both are most useful in winter when other leafy vegetables may be scarce. The only time of year when they will not grow well is in the heat of midsummer, when they are likely to bolt.

Perpetual spinach

Beta vulgaris subsp. *cicla* var. *cicla*

Although perpetual spinach isn't the most attractive plant, it will grow well in even the toughest, most northerly conditions and continually produce nutritious, tasty leaves. In fact it is a biennial and will go on producing leaves well into its second year if allowed to, but for the strongest growth, and the most succulent and tender leaves, make two sowings a year.

	J	F	M	A	M	J	J	A	S	O	N	D
Sow				▪	▪	▪	▪					
Plant					▪	▪						
Harvest					▪	▪	▪	▪	▪	▪	▪	

The best sites and soils

Perpetual spinach tolerates a little shade, particularly in summer, and grows well in moist soil, though it puts up with drier conditions than true spinach. Fertility is important, and you will get stronger growth and better quality leaves if there are lots of nutrients in the soil. Before sowing, dig the ground

COLOUR OR TASTE?

Perpetual spinach is the easiest kind to grow and the most heat-tolerant, but it doesn't have the best flavour. Swiss chard on the other hand (see pages 188-189), with its fantastic range of stem colours, has great ornamental value with a more distinctive flavour. Ordinary spinach (see pages 186-187) is the kind most likely to suffer in the heat, but its superior flavour and texture definitely make it worth the trouble.

over well, adding plenty of well-rotted organic matter and a dressing of general-purpose fertilizer.

Sowing and planting

A spring sowing will keep you in leaves all summer, but the more important sowing is in mid- to late summer, which will produce plants to keep you in leaves all winter long and right into the following early spring. For summer plants, you can sow seed indoors in modules in early spring. Plant outside once the soil has started to warm up. Even easier, just wait until the soil is warm enough to sow direct outside.

If you are growing large leaves for cooking, keep the plants fairly far apart to let them spread. Sow seed in rows 45cm (18in) apart, with 30-38cm (12-15in) between plants, putting a few together as a precaution in case some don't germinate. Good spacing also helps prevent downy mildew, which can occur with poor air circulation if plants are too close together. Seedlings can take a long time to show, often up to a few weeks. When they do appear, thin to leave the strongest in each group. For small leaves in salads, grow as a cut-and-come-again crop. Make

COOKED SPINACH quickly collapses to a surprisingly small amount, so the larger your spinach bed, the better. Thin seedlings to avoid overcrowding and mildew.

a wide drill a few centimetres across, and then scatter seed thinly along and across it, letting the plants grow closer together.

Cultivating the crop

Perpetual spinach can be picked all year round from just two sowings a year. Although it will produce leaves all winter without any special treatment, the leaves are more tender if they have some protection. Either use a polytunnel or cover your row with a cloche or tunnel of fleece. If fleece is simply draped over the plants, it could lead to damaged leaves – in icy weather they can freeze where there is direct contact with the fleece. Some protection is necessary to keep birds off the seedlings.

At harvest time

Leaves are ready for harvesting from eight weeks after sowing; pick them when they have reached the

THE SHINY, CRINKLY LEAVES of fresh spinach are rich in iron and folic acid. Sowing in mid- or late summer provides an excellent supply for the kitchen over winter.

THE CONTAINERIZED VEGETABLE GARDEN. You can pack an amazingly varied range of plants in a decent sized pot, including, as shown, basil, spinach and tomatoes.

required size. On large plants you can either cut the whole plant, or take a few leaves at a time. If you harvest the whole plant, take care not to cut too low down, since this will give the plant the chance to re-sprout. It should do this several times.

To harvest cut-and-come-again crops for salads, hold the tips of a handful of leaves with one hand and use a pair of scissors to cut the base of the leaves. Again, don't cut too low down: leave a little behind so that they can grow again. Harvest leaves for salads when they are still small, even just a few centimetres long, and use them as soon as possible. Harvest little and often, taking only what you need for each meal.

Storing and cooking tips

Leaves will keep for a couple of days in the refrigerator, and can be frozen either before or after being cooked. They need to be cooked for a little longer than true spinach, but still the leaves don't take long to collapse and become tender.

Spinach and swiss chard

" So many people have strong feelings about spinach. You love it or hate it, and I love it. On our market stall many years ago we used to sell our surplus spinach with a big Popeye label to advertise it, and sold out almost as soon as we got there. We then grew perpetual spinach or spinach beet, not annual spinach, because beet does much better here, in fact we can pick it for a full year, sometimes even longer. The aim is to harvest regularly to generate the continuous production of fresh leaves.

Perpetual spinach is closely related to Swiss chard and beetroot. Its leaves are slightly coarser, and more substantial than those of annual spinach. The latter is a fast-growing crop, delicious when young, and it can be eaten raw as a salad or wilted over a gentle heat for a minute at most. Although it is worth growing because it tastes delicious, in hot summers it easily bolts, whereas perpetual spinach and chard seldom do. Even on my substantial soil it takes the first opportunity to flower. It is probably best sown regularly in containers and enjoyed while very young.

CHARD LOOKS AS GOOD as it tastes, and is remarkably easy to grow, tolerating huge amounts of neglect.

Swiss chard has become an essential crop on fashionable vegetable plots, although the striking crimson-leaved variety with its luminous red veins can't hold a torch to the straightforward green-leaved, white-ribbed plant when it comes to flavour. But whichever colour you choose, its aesthetic qualities are always a delight. There are several seed mixes, including 'Rainbow' and 'Bright Lights', with superbly coloured midribs and veins in bright yellow, shocking pink and hot vermillion. It is difficult not to get on your hands and knees on a September evening as the sun sits low in the sky to gaze at your Swiss chard as its stems light up. I can't resist using chard in containers mixed with tropical *Ricinus communis*, purple and red chillies, and tomato-red dahlias.

So full marks for its flamboyant looks, but what about its taste? Well, Swiss chard is a delicacy. Since the leafy part cooks more quickly than the midribs, cook the two separately for different lengths of time (that applies to perpetual spinach). Serve hot with butter, or cold with a dash of olive oil and balsamic vinegar. "

Spinach

Spinacia oleracea

Spinach leaves are among the very best raw in salads. If they're allowed to grow larger, they're delicious lightly cooked. Spinach suffers in summer, and is not as good as perpetual spinach or chard for an all-year crop, but if you give the plant the right conditions, choose the right cultivars, and make successional sowings, you can have fresh leaves all-year round.

	J	F	M	A	M	J	J	A	S	O	N	D
Sow			▪	▪	▪	▪	▪	▪				
Harvest			▪	▪	▪	▪	▪	▪	▪		▪	

The best sites and soils

Spinach has the same requirements as perpetual spinach (see page 182), but note that spinach is a prima donna, refusing to perform if conditions are not right. It needs plenty of moisture at the roots and lots of nutrients, so apply a general fertilizer and do not attempt to grow it in dry soil with low fertility. Add plenty of well-rotted manure or compost to the soil before sowing, and providing a little shade in summer will help, as this will keep the ground cool and moist. Also consider intercropping with taller vegetables that will cast a dappled shade over the spinach during the midday heat. Spinach suffers from few soil-borne problems and can be grown anywhere in your rotation. However, downy mildew can be troublesome in warm, humid weather. Avoid congested plants and use resistant varieties where possible.

Sowing and planting

If you like spinach, be generous with your sowing so that you can gather great handfuls for the steamer or wok – it cooks down to almost nothing. Sow the seed

Recommended varieties

Scenic AGM
A high-yielding variety with large, bright green leaves that is particularly suitable as a cut-and-come again crop. Resistant to mildew

Bordeaux
Very attractive dark green leaves with contrasting red leaf veins and stems make this a good baby spinach for salads.

Toscane AGM
A late-maturing spinach with smooth, good-looking leaves and high yields. Slow to bolt.

Medania AGM
Bulks up reliably with slightly blistered, large round leaves. Slow to bolt even in hot weather.

TO GET THE YEAR'S FIRST CROP of spinach, sow after mid-spring but no later than the start of summer because the seed won't germinate once there's hot weather.

directly where it is to grow in drills about 1cm (½in) deep in rows 30cm (12in) apart. Since spinach will not easily germinate in hot weather, and tends to bolt if sown too early, make sowings from mid-spring to early summer for summer leaves, and then in autumn for a supply of leaves into winter. Despite this, it is possible, if you are determined, to get leaves all-year round if you give plants the right conditions and choose the right varieties. Make successive sowings of small amounts of seed every few weeks for a continuous supply of fresh leaves.

To grow large plants, sow small clumps of a few seeds at least 15cm (6in) apart. Thin to one seedling in each group once all have germinated. To grow small salad leaves, make a wide drill and scatter the seed thinly across it. You should not need to thin the seedlings.

At harvest time

Keep well watered at all times to stop the plants bolting to seed at the expense of the leaves. Once a plant has bolted, there's not much you can do

EVERY SPINACH LOVER'S NIGHTMARE. A spinach bed sown too early in the year, right at the start of spring, resulting in wasted, bolted plants which quickly flower.

except pull it up. Remove weeds regularly, and apply a mulch to lock moisture in the ground. If the vigour of the plants seems to be failing, then apply a nitrogen-rich fertilizer following the manufacturer's instructions. Where birds are a problem, then you may have to grow spinach under a net.

Storage and cooking tips

Spinach is the gourmet plant of the group, producing delicately flavoured, soft-textured leaves that are particularly good when raw.

Whatever size of leaves you harvest, put them straight into a plastic bag to keep them fresh and succulent. Store in the fridge as soon as possible until you need them. Spinach can be successfully frozen either cooked or raw.

Leaves can be steamed before being eaten or stir-fried. If you enjoy cooked spinach, remember that the leaves collapse down to almost nothing once heated, so be generous with your sowing so that you can gather great handfuls when the time comes for the steamer or wok.

Pests and diseases

Apart from the usual preventative measures against slugs and snails, which will devour emerging seedlings, birds are also likely to attack a young crop. If they are a problem, then cover the young crop with netting. Spinach is also vulnerable to downy mildew. Either give extra space to your crops to improve ventialtion or grow a resistant variety.

Swiss chard

Beta vulgaris subsp. *cicla* var. *flavescens*

Swiss chard's colourful stems – yellow, pink, red, white and orange – are its big attraction in a salad or cooking pot. And that colour means it can be used to edge a vegetable bed, or perk up a mixed border. It is more tolerant of heat than spinach, and will grow well through summer, but is more likely to make it to the kitchen table in winter when its colour is most welcome.

	J	F	M	A	M	J	J	A	S	O	N	D
Sow				▪	▪	▪	▪	▪				
Plant					▪	▪						
Harvest	▪	▪	▪	▪	▪	▪	▪	▪	▪	▪	▪	▪

The best sites and soils

Swiss chard is ideally grown in an open site, on fertile, moist soil. It can keep producing for a long time, so it's particularly important that you improve the soil before planting if you are planning to leave the plants in the ground over a long period instead of making successive sowings through the year.

Sowing and planting

When growing single plants to produce large leaves for cooking, sow the seed in a seed tray and plant out the seedlings once they have germinated. Space them about 45cm (18in) apart. Sow in late spring for summer and autumn picking, and in late summer for a winter crop, although the first sowing will often carry on producing well into winter. Sowings for cut-and-come-again plants should be made direct in the

SWISS CHARD comes in such a flashy, startling range of colours that it's often given a prime spot at the front of a flower bed.

WHEN HARVESTING YELLOW CHARD, use sharp secateurs to snip away the leaves, not cutting too close to the plant.

ground using the same timings. Make a wide drill and sow the seeds thinly across it.

Cultivating the crop

Swiss chard is one of the easiest vegetables to grow. It takes any amount of neglect and still looks good and produces leaves. Weed and keep the soil moist during dry weather for the best leaves, but the plant will withstand some drought once it's established. Over winter you will get the best-quality crop if you cover the plants with cloches to protect them from the worst of the weather. Plants may bolt in warmer weather or if they are not regularly cut, but they are so vigorous that they can just be chopped back and they will start producing good, tasty leaves again.

At harvest time

Harvest large leaves for cooking individually as you need them, but do not cut too close to the plant.

You can also cut the whole plant for cooking but, again, make the cut 5cm (2in) up the stem so that the plant can re-sprout. It will do this several times.

With plants that are not covered over winter, the outer leaves may be damaged, in which case you can just harvest the inner ones, leaving the outer ones as protection against the elements.

Storing and cooking tips

Large leaves can also be frozen, raw or having been cooked, but do not freeze leaves for salad. Large leaves can be steamed whole, but the tougher leaf stalks take longer to cook than the more tender leaves. Ideally they should be cooked separately, or the leaf stalk should be chopped up and added to the steamer a few minutes before the leaves are added. Both then take just a few minutes.

Recommended varieties

Bright Lights AGM
This is a good, colourful mixture of reliable varieties, including reds, yellows and whites. Very ornamental and decorative.

Rhubarb Chard AGM
The strikingly deep-red leaf stalks of this variety are a good uniform colour and the yields are high. A very pretty leaf crop.

Squashes, marrows, pumpkins and sweetcorn

Although summer and winter squashes and sweetcorn are not related, they make excellent companions. Squashes and corns come from Central and South America where they have been cultivated for thousands of years. Like pumpkins and marrows, they grow best in long hot summers, and enjoy the sunniest position in the vegetable patch. Seeds need to be sown and grown in a frost-free environment (a greenhouse or sunny windowsill), and can be planted out only when all risk of frost has passed and – ideally – the soil has started to warm up.

Courgettes, marrows and summer squashes

" For quick results and a bumper yield, courgettes, summer squashes and marrows must win first prize. Raise them with some protection to get an early start, but from the moment the first seedlings push their twin leaves through the compost it is clear that this is a plant to be reckoned with. The seeds themselves are substantial. Each is best

sown individually on its side, pushed into friable seed compost in a separate pot. In a warm place it will germinate in days. Seed can be sown as early as March but the plants grow vigorously and may have run out of steam by midsummer, so be prepared to sow more to keep generating a crop into autumn.

All members of the cucurbit family enjoy rich soil, so when the plants go out into their final positions the ground should be full of moisture-retaining muck or compost. And because they are succulent plants, loved by slugs, don't put the plants out until they have a fighting chance. The flowers and fruit are both edible, but with the exception of marrows, the fruit is best when young and small. The fruits grow very quickly, with the sweet flavour dissipating as the fruit expands. When in full growth, inspect the courgette and summer squash plants everyday. Leave them for a few days and you may be faced with a multitude of overgrown squash or marrows.

Courgettes and summer squash should be eaten as soon as they are ready and can be cooked in many ways. For the most part, recipes are simple and quick – try flowers and diced fruit in a risotto. Marrows may develop attractively striped skins and can be hollowed out and stuffed with diced vegetables. "

COURGETTES, MARROWS AND SQUASHES are incredibly prolific, and keep pumping out first-rate fruit right through summer.

Courgettes, marrows and summer squashes

Cucurbita pepo

Even a single plant in this easy-to-grow and highly productive group will produce fantastic yields. 'Courgette' usually refers to the long, cylindrical fruits with green or yellow skin. Summer squash are similar to courgettes but have different shapes and textures. Marrows are botanically the same as courgettes but mature into longer, more rounded and handsome fruits.

	J	F	M	A	M	J	J	A	S	O	N	D
Sow				■	■	■						
Plant					■	■						
Harvest							■	■	■	■	■	

The best sites and soils

All this group thrive in hot summers and need the sunniest position available. They are at their best in fertile, moist soil. Any type of soil is fine as the plants are very robust. A good site can be improved by the addition of plenty of manure or garden compost, as well as a dressing of general fertilizer, which helps to increase the soil's ability to retain moisture.

THREE-CROP COOPERATION

Summer and winter squashes and sweetcorn constitute two-thirds of the 'three sisters' growing system developed by American Indian farmers (see page 8). The squashes cover the ground, smothering weeds and keeping the soil cool and moist, while the corn towers above. Because they have differing growth habits they do not compete for space, and both get adequate sunlight. The third member of the trio is the bean, which clambers up the corn stalk, but this works only if you are growing both beans and corn for drying, and can harvest by chopping the whole lot down at the end of the season.

Sowing and planting

Although marrows can be considered to be courgettes grown large, if you are intending to grow marrows, it is better to select a marrow cultivar rather than a courgette as the resulting fruit will be easier to use. Courgettes are notorious for producing an unmanageable glut all at once. Two plants (they take up quite a lot of space) should keep you supplied without gluts.

Sow seed under cover and in bright conditions, about one month before the last predicted frost. Early sowing indoors or out is rarely of much benefit as the seeds may not germinate if the soil is too cold, or cold temperatures may damage young plants. Since the large seedlings do not transplant well, sow them

A COURGETTE PLANT takes up a big chunk of space, but if there's no room in the vegetable garden, raise it in a growbag, placed where convenient, but full sun is a must.

individually into small pots to minimize root disturbance. Harden off and plant out when the seedlings have two or three leaves. Outdoors, sow where they are to grow, two seeds per station, thinning as soon as possible to one seedling. Outdoor sowings often overtake indoor-raised plants.

If the soil is very poor, dig a planting hole to about a spade's depth, width and height. Mix lots of well-rotted manure or compost from a growbag into the soil before you refill the hole. Courgette plants tend to be quite compact and bushy, and should be spaced about 90cm (3ft) apart.

Summer squashes and marrows are more likely to be trailing plants, and can take up much more room, needing spacings up to 1.8m (6ft). Laying down a polythene mulch, and then cutting planting holes in it, will help retain moisture in the ground and suppress weeds. However, plastic is a breeding ground for slugs, so be vigilant if you use this method, particularly when

THE BULBOUS FRUITS of marrow are easier to stuff than courgettes and keep well if sun-ripened.

COURGETTES ARE FORMIDABLE GUZZLERS in hot weather, and should never be allowed to dry out in summer when new fruit is developing. Regular drinks guarantee quality fruit.

the plants are small and vulnerable to attack. Another alternative is to place a mulch over the surface after watering the plant in well. In the variable and often cool weather of spring, plants benefit from the protection of a cloche. Once the weather is reliably warm, the cloche can be removed.

Cultivating the crop

Where space is limited, check the spread of trailing types by pinning down the growth in a circle, or training them over a sturdy support, tying the plants in regularly as they grow.

As the fruit starts to form, feed the pot-grown plants. Use a liquid fertilizer every week or two. If outdoor plants fail to thrive, sprinkle nitrogen-rich fertilizer near the base of the plant and water in. Watering is most important as the fruit is starting to form; the more the plants are watered at this time, the better quality the fruit will be. Water plants generously every

THE TASTIEST COURGETTES are picked when young and thin. Slice them off using a sharp kitchen knife. Never try the twist-and-pull approach as it will damage the plant.

10 days in dry spells, being sure to soak the soil well. Too much water leaves the plants open to powdery mildew. Although sulphur dust will slow the spread of this disease, it is better to avoid it in the first place.

At harvest time

Always use a sharp knife to cut courgettes and summer squashes cleanly from the plant. If you are tempted to try to twist or pull the fruit off, you will invariably damage the plant or the fruit. They should be young and tender, about 13cm (5in) long. If left, they'll quickly grow much larger, losing flavour and becoming watery as they do so. Marrow size is less critical to flavour. As a rule, marrows are ready when about 20–30cm (8–12in) long, or they can be left to mature for winter use.

Recommended varieties (courgettes)

Venus AGM
Compact plant with a bumper crop over a long season of dark green fruit. A reliable performer with smooth, spine-free stems.

Black Forest
Climbing cultivar for training over an arch or trellis. This unusual growth habit for a courgette makes it good for small spaces. Good yields and suits containers.

Recommended varieties (marrows)

Tiger Cross AGM
A very fetching striped marrow with high yields of relatively early fruits. They are good for winter storage and there is reported resistance to cucumber mosaic virus.

Badger Cross AGM
Similar to 'Tiger Cross' but with later yields. Distinctive dark-skinned, small but perfectly formed fruit with pale green stripes. Some resistance to cucumber mosaic virus.

Storing and cooking tips

The differences between the courgettes, marrows and squashes are not always clear cut, but there are basically two main groups: those grown to be eaten young and fresh in summer, and those grown until their skin toughens into autumn, making them suitable for winter storage.

Summer squash can be lightly barbecued and sprinkled with fresh mint and olive oil, and is one of the essential tastes of the season. When picked tiny it can even be eaten raw in a salad. The flowers can also be eaten raw or cooked, and are sometimes stuffed, dipped in a light batter and deep-fried. Summer squash will store for only a few days, and once picked must be kept in a refrigerator where it

POLLINATION

In cool summers you may notice that fruit is not setting, which is due to inadequate pollination, and this may be remedied by removing a male flower and brushing the central parts against the centre of a female flower. Female flowers are easy to identify because they have a small fruit behind them, but male flowers do not.

will last for up to a week, to keep it hydrated and in good condition.

Marrow has a reputation for tasting bland, but certain cultivars have denser, less watery flesh than others. Marrows can be eaten fresh or stored for a month or two. They can be stuffed (for example with rice mixed with cheese and vegetables, or minced beef with tomatoes and herbs) and baked. 'Spaghetti marrow' looks like ordinary marrow but has tough skin and its flesh forms spaghetti-like strands.

Courgettes can be kept fresh in the refrigerator for a few days, but will not store for very long, and need to be eaten soon after harvest.

COURGETTE FLOWERS are quite a delicacy, and need to be picked just as they are opening, going straight into the kitchen. They can be stuffed and fried in batter.

WHEN HARVESTING SUMMER SQUASH, it is best to wear gloves in order to protect your hands from the spines. It is also advisable to use secateurs to avoid damage to the plants.

Winter squashes and pumpkins

❝ Children love pumpkins. The idea that a small seed can change into a monster is thrilling. It's almost like keeping a pet. The pumpkins that are grown for Hallowe'en, as big and orange as can be, are just one variety of a very diverse group, which includes winter squashes. All pumpkins are cucurbits – vine-like fruits with hollow stems, immense leaves and extensive growth. They are explorers constantly questing to find space to open their flowers and set fruit. The flowers themselves are reason enough to grow the plant.

With the exception of a few cucumbers, all cucurbits have both male and female flowers. It is obvious which is which: the male flowers concentrate on producing stamens bearing the rich golden pollen to pollinate their opposite numbers, and each female flower has an embryonic fruit behind it, which begins to swell once pollinated.

Plants grow rapidly, which is ideal if you need a quick cover-up, but more of a problem if space is at a premium. Growing smaller fruiting pumpkins and squashes up a temporary support, such as a big,

BY FAR THE MOST IMPRESSIVE vegetables you'll ever grow are huge winter squashes and pumpkins. Go on. Have a go.

chunky obelisk or pergola, allows the fruit to hang down. If they get too big, support them with nets tied to the structure. Big pumpkins and squashes are best on the ground. As they swell and ripen, the fruits need a clay tile or a big clay plant pot to prop them up and allow the skin to ripen evenly. The thick skins can be so tough that you can feel you need a machete to hack into them, but they ensure that the contents remain in perfect condition for months.

While the fruit is the talking point, especially the immense orange footballs of 'Atlantic Giant' and the warty fruit of 'Marina di Chioggia', the proof of the pudding is in the eating, and the most important aspect of any vegetable is its taste. It is here that winter squashes prove their merit, as the flesh is usually nutty and much sweeter. Popular types include the acorns, butternuts and the blue-skinned 'Crown Prince', but scour the Internet and seed catalogues for other varieties to see if you can find something really special. ❞

Winter squashes and pumpkins

Cucurbita maxima

They're just what you want in your larder as the weather turns cold: perfectly cured fruits, all wonderfully autumnal, worth growing for their looks alone. Pumpkins in general are not as tasty as winter squashes, which come in all shapes and sizes from the round and onion-like to the long and thin, with skin colours including blue, deep orange, pale yellow and dark green.

	J	F	M	A	M	J	J	A	S	O	N	D
Sow				■	■	■						
Plant					■	■						
Harvest								■	■	■	■	

The best sites and soils

Long, hot summers are ideal in fertile, moist soil. Provide the sunniest, most sheltered spot and improve the soil before planting with general-purpose fertilizer.

TO GROW A GIANT PUMPKIN, leave one fruit on the plant. Water well, feed and protect from pests by sitting it on a brick.

Sowing and planting

Since winter squashes and pumpkins need a long, hot growing season to ripen fully, look for cultivars that are early ripening. You must also time your seed-sowing to give plants the maximum growing time outdoors. Since plants are frost-tender, you must sow seed indoors or in a frost-free greenhouse about one month before the last expected frost.

Plant out when the risk of frost has passed. Water in and mulch the soil, and erect a cloche or cover with fleece if the weather turns really chilly.

Cultivating the crop

Apply liquid fertilizer every couple of weeks, or scatter chicken manure pellets around the plant soon after planting. It should be necessary to water only during particularly hot and dry spells. If you are growing large cultivars, remove the growing tip once three fruits have set, since this gives them a better chance of ripening. If your main aim is to grow the largest possible pumpkin or squash, leave one fruit on each plant and give it extra water and feed. As the fruit swells, place it on pieces of wood or brick to keep it off the wet soil and avoid pest attacks.

At harvest time

Fruit for eating fresh can be cut off the plant as required, but if it's to store well over winter it must be fully ripened and cured. Leave the fruit on the plant for as long as possible and it should develop a tough skin that will prevent rotting for up to six months, depending on the

SEEDS FROM A PUMPKIN or squash can be extracted from the vegetable by crushing it and cutting it open. Soak the seeds in water to remove the pulp, then dry out and store.

TRAILING TYPES CAN BE GROWN UP supports – greenhouses providing an excellent opportunity – but the supports must be strong to take the weight.

variety. There follows a fine balancing act as you try to keep the fruit on the plant, but avoid exposing it to frost since a hard frost will make the flesh turn mushy. If in doubt, cover the fruits with cardboard or straw. Winter squashes may lack flavour if harvested too early. Because of the vast varieties of sizes and colours, the rule of thumb is to wait until they are a full size, have a deep rich colour and the rinds are hard to the touch.

When you decide the fruit is adequately ripened, cut it off the plant, taking with it as much of the stalk as possible. Since rot starts from the stalk end, the longer

MAXIMIZING YIELDS

Pumpkins and squashes like lots of nutrients and water, and they are often planted out on old compost heaps. This gives fantastically healthy plants, although robust varieties usually do well on any good garden soil. Digging out a large planting hole and incorporating lots of well-rotted manure or grow-bag compost might be necessary for really poor soils. Feed with tomato fertilizer every two weeks.

PUMPKINS AND SQUASHES need a long, hot growing season and so benefit from being grown indoors away from the risk of frost.

Recommended varieties (pumpkins)

Becky
A classic orange, medium-sized Hallowe'en pumpkin that is perfect for carving. Very prolific and high yielding. 'Hundredweight' is a similar but much larger variety. Trailing habit.

Rouge Vif d'Etamps
A really stunning pumpkin with red, ribbed skin and moist orange flesh. They are very ornamental in the autumn, both in the garden and indoors. The growth is vigorous and trailing.

Recommended varieties (winter squashes)

Crown Prince
A recognizable trailing squash with blue skin and orange flesh and a sweet nutty flavour. The yields are good and the large fruit store well over winter if kept cool and dry.

Cobnut
One of the earliest maturing butternut pumpkins, suitable for cooler climates as it has longer to ripen. Produces a reliable crop of delicious fruits that are ideal for roasting or making soups. Trailing habit.

the stalk, the longer rotting is delayed. Do not be tempted, however, to use the long stalk as a handle, as this risks damage to the fruit. Once the fruit has been cut from the plant, it needs a further ten days to cure. Ideally, this should be in full sun outside, but weather at this time of year is unpredictable, so it often has to be done indoors. Alternatively, cure it in a greenhouse, polytunnel or cold frame, where the fruit gets warmth and light without getting wet.

Storing and cooking tips

Once it is well cured, store the fruit in a dry place with temperatures under 15°C (60°F). Never store your fruit where there is a risk of freezing. If you have a large crop, don't stack them too high as they need plenty of air to breathe so they don't prematurely rot. Another option is to cut your fruit into chunks and to freeze them; but it is advisable to use your frozen fruit quickly to maintain flavour. Although it can be eaten immediately, winter squash goes down best during the coldest months when the garden produces little else. It is a real treat to pull out a large, heavy fruit and slice into it, revealing

WINTER SQUASHES should be cured for ten days in full sun outside, as long as it stays dry, or indoors in a greenhouse, polytunnel or cold frame.

TO GROW LARGE PUMPKINS or squashes, leave one fruit on each plant and give it extra water and feed.

the dense, orange flesh inside. The large ones are best chopped into chunks and roasted in oil and garlic until slightly caramelized, while smaller ones can be baked whole and eaten with a knob of butter and a shake of salt and pepper.

Pumpkins are often grown for decorative purposes, many being used for carved faces at Hallowe'en. Some produce seed that's good for roasting and eating, and a few varieties, such as 'Jack Be Little' and 'Rouge Vif d'Etamps' combine good looks and the sweet taste that characterize rich, warming, golden pumpkin soups.

Sweetcorn

" Although sweetcorn has been grown since man began cultivating the land, sweetcorn as we know it was developed in the 19th century. Recent advances in breeding mean it tastes even better now, with sweeter kernels and varieties whose sugar content stays high for longer.

WITH GARDENS becoming increasingly fun and inventive, try growing sweetcorn to the front of a border for dramatic effect.

Harvested at its peak, the flavour is superlative. Grasp the stem with one hand and push the fat cob downwards. With a satisfying crack it snaps off cleanly from the stem. Then peel down the outside casing exposing the plump golden kernels stacked on top of each other in a tightly packed cylinder. Strip off any remnants of the tassel and plunge the cob into boiling water. In a few minutes it is cooked to perfection. Drain and, as soon as it is cool enough to hold, eat.

Because fast-maturing sweetcorn is a tender crop, it will be damaged if planted out before the last serious frosts in late spring. It makes rapid progress once it takes off and needs a relatively short growing season. In mid-spring, sow in modules or small individual but deep pots in a greenhouse or on a windowsill, one or two seeds per compartment. When the seedlings are a few inches high, pot on into bigger pots. It is worth repeating this using bigger pots until each plant is strong and sturdy, especially in colder parts of the country. Sweetcorn hates root disturbance but this way its roots fill each pot in turn and the rootball stays intact. When all danger of frost has passed, the plants can be put out to face the big wide world. Not too much of a shock though – sweetcorn love each other's company and need to be planted in a block rather than in lines or individually. Since they are pollinated by the wind, planting them close to one another ensures that the pollen produced on the apical heads of the male flowers ends up on the female flowers – the tassels borne halfway down the stems – which will eventually swell to produce the cob. "

Sweetcorn *Zea mays*

There is an enormous difference between a freshly harvested cob and one that has been stored. The sugars start turning to starch as soon as a cob is picked, and it quickly loses its tenderness and tastiness. No matter how hard they try, supermarkets and greengrocers can't compete with a cob that has been harvested, boiled and eaten within the hour.

	J	F	M	A	M	J	J	A	S	O	N	D
Sow				■	■	■						
Plant					■	■						
Harvest								■	■	■	■	

The best sites and soils

Choose a sheltered, sunny site for planting. Sweetcorn is not fussy about soil, and will grow well provided the soil is well drained and has average fertility. If in doubt, dress with a general fertilizer.

Sowing and planting

Supersweet varieties are thought to have the sweetest taste and the most tender, juicy kernels. If you choose to cultivate these you mustn't also grow the older cultivars, which are still available, because cross pollination causes the kernels to turn starchy.

Sweetcorn needs a warm season with no hint of frost for its fruit to mature. This means for an early crop in cold areas you should sow the seed indoors and plant out when all danger of frost has gone. Supersweet cultivars are more difficult to germinate and the seed is more likely to rot in cool, damp conditions. Use a heated propagator if you have one.

Sow each seed into a large module or small pot to avoid root disturbance when planting out the seedlings. Each plant produces a couple of cobs, and a block of plants is enough for most people. When transplanting, spacing the young plants is crucial, as only pollinated kernels will swell. Male flowers shower pollen down from the top of the plant to the females below which capture it. Pollination is most successful when plants are grown in blocks, because the pollen is less likely to be blown away from the female flowers and more likely to land on its target. Make blocks at least four

BABY CORN

When planting for baby corn, plant in rows, not blocks, to avoid the corn being pollinated and starting to swell. Plant much closer together, at gaps of about 20cm (8in). The corn must be planted slightly more deeply to encourage the growth of extra roots above the normal ones, to help stabilize the plant and prevent wind rock. In a cool spring, cover young plants with fleece until the weather warms up.

plants deep and wide, with each plant 35–45cm (15–18in) apart. For a successful crop in warm areas, sow the seeds where they are to grow in late spring and early summer.

Cultivating the crop

Watering is particularly key while the plants are getting established and as the kernels are swelling, although it should not be necessary to water much in between, except during particularly hot, dry weather. Otherwise, cultivation is simply a matter of keeping the area around the plants weed-free. You could also mulch the plants once they are established. If you notice them starting to rock in high winds, earth them up to foster the growth of stabilizing adventitious roots.

At harvest time

Sweetcorn starts to mature from midsummer on. Once the tassels on the ends of the cobs turn brown you can start testing for maturity. Peel back the husk to check the corn: it will be pale yellow when ready to be picked, and a milky liquid will appear when a kernel is pricked. It is vital to pick the cobs when they have just reached

EARTHING UP SWEETCORN

1 AS WELL AS MULCHING the sweetcorn, you should add some more earth around the plants if your site is exposed to strong winds.

2 GENTLY SCOOP the new earth around the base of each plant, protecting them from damage and encouraging the growth of adventitious roots.

ripeness, or they will not be at their best. Baby corn (obtained by planting normal corn at close spacings), should be harvested before the cobs are mature.

Storing and cooking tips

Sweetcorn does not store well, although it can be eaten a few days later if kept refrigerated. Pick only what you want to eat that day, preferably as close to cooking time as possible.

Pick baby corn when it is just a few centimetres long and eat raw or lightly cooked. Throw it into a pan of

boiling water for a few minutes, drain, and serve with butter and a little salt and pepper. Cobs that are grown for drying should be left on the plant beyond ripeness, until they start to dry on the plant. You can then harvest and continue to dry them indoors. Hang them in an airy spot for a few weeks. They will only pop well if they are completely dry (some cultivars make better popcorn than others) so when they're ready, test a few kernels in a pan of hot oil first. Once they are fully dried they can be stored in airtight jars for several months. Remove the kernels and cook in hot oil, or place the whole cob in the microwave.

Recommended varieties

Lark AGM
A fairly early maturing, extra tender sweet variety with bright, uniformly yellow, soft-textured kernels. The growth is reasonably vigorous and the cobs are large.

Swift AGM
An early maturing, extra tender, sweet, medium-sized variety. It is said to grow well in cool climates. The cobs are uniformly yellow with a deliciously sweet flavour.

Tender vegetables